DIAMONDS . . . *Famous, Notable and Unique*

Books by the Same Publishers

DICTIONARY OF GEMS & GEMOLOGY
Robert M. Shipley

THE JEWELERS' MANUAL
Lawrence L. Copeland, Richard T. Liddicoat, Jr.

HANDBOOK OF GEM IDENTIFICATION
Richard T. Liddicoat, Jr.

THE DIAMOND DICTIONARY
Lawrence L. Copeland, Richard T. Liddicoat, Jr.,
Lester B. Benson, Jr., Jeanne G. M. Martin,
G. Robert Crowningshield

DIAMONDS . . . *Famous, Notable and Unique*

Nepal Diamond. 79.41 carats. Courtesy Harry Winston, Inc., New York City

DIAMONDS...

Famous, Notable and Unique

by
LAWRENCE L. COPELAND

Course Editor and Research Librarian

with
Artwork, Design and Photography

by
JEANNE G. M. MARTIN

Publications Manager

Revised by
R. A. P. GAAL, Ph.D.
Research Scientist

and
JIM TAYLOR
Diamond Correspondence Course Supervisor

Published by

GEMOLOGICAL INSTITUTE OF AMERICA

Preface

The purpose of this book is to provide the reader with entertaining, factual accounts of the great and near-great diamonds of history — not only those that have gained worldwide fame because of their historical background, but those that are worthy of attention because of significant size or rarity or even uniqueness of color, crystal shape, phenomenal properties, method of fashioning or unusual source. It is also intended to serve as reference material for jewelers, lecturers and researchers.

During the research for the book, an effort was made to assemble and present pertinent historical information gathered from every possible reliable source; to bring earlier records of historical fact up to date with verification from archivists, museum curators, gemologists and present owners; and to add hitherto unknown facts and stories that were made available for publication by these persons.

Few works have been written on this subject. The principal publications are *The Great Diamonds of the World,* by Edwin W. Streeter (1882); *Famous Diamonds of the World,* by Robert M. Shipley (1948); *Famous Diamonds,* by Ian Balfour, De Beers Consolidated Mines, Ltd. (early 1960's); and *The Histories of Some Famous Diamonds,* by Kathleen C. Horan, N. W. Ayer & Son, Inc. (1965). The present volume is based partially on the descriptions of thirty-one historic diamonds embodied in Shipley's work; for this useful background information the author is deeply indebted.

Numerous persons and organizations have contributed materially to this writing project, by furnishing both information and photographs. Noteworthy among those who have given their wholehearted cooperation and assistance are the following:

DIAMONDS . . . *Famous, Notable and Unique*

American Museum of Natural History, New York City; the Third Viscount Astor, Maidenhead, Berks, England; Joseph Baumgold, Baumgold Bros., Inc., New York City; William A. Burns, Ph.D., Witte Memorial Museum, San Antonio, Texas; G. F. Claringbull, Ph.D., Keeper of Minerals, British Museum of Natural History, London; Julius Cohen, Inc., New York City; *Musée de Condé,* Chantilly, France; Robert Crowningshield, Director, Gemological Institute of America, New York City; Lady Lydia Deterding, Paris, France; Thomas Draper, São Paulo, Brazil; Myron Everts, President, Arthur A. Everts Co., Dallas, Texas; Dr. Herman Fillitz, *Kunsthistorisches* Museum, Vienna, Austria; Arthur Fine, Max Fine & Sons, Inc., New York City; Dr. W. Fleischhauer, Director, Wurttemburg *Landsmuseum,* Stuttgart, Germany; Joseph Freeman, Freeman-Lewis, Inc., New York City; Daniel Frey, Harry Winston, Inc., New York City; Marcel Ginsburg, E. Sévery-M. Ginsburg, Antwerp, Belgium; Charles A. Golding, Her Majesty's Stationery Office, London, England; Michael Grantham, De Beers Consolidated Mines, Ltd., London, England; Kathleen C. Horan, N. W. Ayer & Son, New York City; George Kaplan, Lazare Kaplan & Sons, New York City; J. Komkommer, I. Komkommer & Zn., N. V. Antwerp, Belgium; Mrs. William B. Leeds, New York City; Harry A. Levinson, Levinson's, Inc., Chicago, Illinois; William T. Lusk, President, Tiffany & Co., New York City; Dr. J. Menzhausen, Green Vaults, State Art Collection, Historical Museum, Dresden, Germany; Morris S. Nelkin, New York City; Hayrullah Örs, *Topkapi Muzesi Mudurlugu,* Istanbul, Turkey; Esmeraldino Ries, Departamento Nacional da Produção Mineral, Divisão de Geologia, Rio de Janeiro, Brazil; Meyer Rosenbaum, Meyer Jewelry Co., Detroit, Michigan; Medhi Samii, Governor, the Central Bank of Iran, Tehran; Dr. José López Sánchez, Scientific Secretary, Comision Nacional de la Academia de Ciencias de la República de Cuba, Havana; George Switzer, Chairman, Department of Mineral Sciences, Smithsonian Institution, Washington, D.C.; Mary Vandegrift, Vice President, Parke-Bernet Galleries, Inc., New York City; Pierre Verlet,

Preface

Louvre Museum, Paris, France; Paul-Louis Weiller, Paris, France; Jack M. Werst, Miami, Florida; and Charles F. Winson, Inc., New York City.

In addition, much valuable and friendly assistance has come from United States consulates and foreign consular representatives, both in this country and abroad.

Lastly, the author wishes to express his heartfelt appreciation to Jeanne G.M. Martin, Manager of GIA's Publication Department, and Richard T. Liddicoat, Jr., Executive Director of the Institute, without whose critical comments and valuable assistance in all areas of the project this book would not have been possible. Miss Martin was responsible for the scratch drawings, format and layout; equally important, she photographed all of the glass replicas of famous diamonds. Liddicoat acted in the capacity of supervising editor, making many important suggestions relative to both picture selection and text.

March, 1966   LLC

Preface to Revised Edition

This book, as with the preceding edition, maintains its original purpose. Since the last edition, new and additional information and many new diamonds have appeared which needed inclusion in the text. The general organization of the book remains the same, except that a new section containing up-to-date information on "Recent and Additional Important Diamonds" has been added to the Appendix in alphabetical order for easy reference.

We have been fortunate to have had the consultive assistance of the GIA staff in the preparation of the manuscript for this edition. We are greatly indebted to R. T. Liddicoat, Jr., for over-all editorial guidance and advice, and to Sue Adams for her skill and care in typing, reading and proofing the text. Rose Levine contributed greatly with proofing and criticism. Also, we would like to thank N. W. Ayer & Son, Inc., for their generous help, especially Gene Laroff and Florence McDermott.

November, 1974   R. A. P. G.

Akbar Shah

HE celebrated *Akbar Shah Diamond* once belonged to Shah Jehan, the Indian ruler famous for building the Taj Mahal, and presumably to his grandfather, Akbar Shah, the most illustrious of India's Mogul emperors. The *Akbar Shah* is remarkable for its Arabic inscriptions, which indicated ownership. The first engraved marking read, "Shah Akbar, the Shah of the World, 1028, A.H." (the letters mean "After Hegira," the first year of the Moslem era, A.D. 622, which would correspond to our 1650). However, since Akbar died in 1605, he could not have made the engraving. The date of 1650 is obviously when Shah Jehan had it made, and the inscription merely means that Akbar once owned the stone.

The second inscription ("To the Lord of Two Worlds, 1039 A.H. Shah Jehan") apparently was added eleven years later by Jehan, whose reign (1628-1658) covered both dates. Since it can be assumed that he was responsible for both inscriptions, the latter indicates that Jehan was somewhat egotistical!

The *Akbar Shah* was probably among the many treasures taken by Persia's Nadir Shah during his sack of Delhi in 1739. The pillage and destruction that this beautiful city suffered at Nadir's hands was almost without parallel. With no warning whatever, this warrior-prince descended on Delhi. He plundered its great palaces and annihilated his opponents. Amidst the fire and smoke of its devastated public buildings, he removed his booty with abandon; nothing of value was spared. The bejeweled Peacock Throne, the treasures of the wealthy, and even the ordinary possessions of the laborer were included in the indiscriminate loot.

1

DIAMONDS . . .

Akbar Shah Diamond (glass
replica). 71.70 carats. GIA
Photo

Engraved markings on Akbar Shah Diamond.
71.70 carats

The storied *Koh-i-Noor Diamond* and the coveted *Darya-i-Nur Diamond*, together with wagonloads of less valuable objects, were removed *en masse* to Khurasan. There, Nadir arrayed himself in the spoils of his royal victim and, unconsciously, by his triumph, paved the way for his murder and the destruction of his own dynasty.

According to legend, the *Akbar Shah* was one of the eyes of the priceless Peacock Throne, the construction of which was begun by Shah Jehan and completed by

Aurungzeb, his son. The Throne represented, in appropriate jewels, a peacock with its head overlooking, and its raised and spread tail overshadowing, the seated emperor. The natural hues of the bird were exquisitely imitated by the costliest gems of the world.

For more than a century, the whereabouts of the diamond was a mystery. Finally, in 1886, it was purchased in Constantinople (where it was called the *Shepherd Stone*) by George Blogg, a London merchant, who recut it from its original 116 carats to a 71.70-carat drop shape. The inscriptions, which were of historic rather than decorative value, were destroyed in the recutting.

Although the stone is known to have been sold to the Gaekwar of Baroda in 1867 for about $175,000, it can only be presumed that ownership of the *Akbar Shah* remains unchanged today. Efforts to establish its present location by the Gemological Institute of America have been to no avail.

Anton Dunkels' Necklace

NTON DUNKELS, a distinguished diamond merchant and head of the firm of A. Dunkelsbuhler & Co. in the early days of the South African diamond fields, gave this necklace its name. Composed of large (size unknown) fancy-colored and black-diamond drops, it is one of the world's most notable pieces of jewelry neckwear.

In 1959, the piece was one of the features of the *Ageless Diamond Exhibition* in London, sponsored jointly by De Beers Consolidated Mines, Ltd., and Christie, Manson & Woods, the famous London auction house.

Archduke Joseph

N June, 1961, a diamond that formerly belonged to Archduke Joseph of Austria came up for auction at the well-known London auction house of Sotheby's. It was described as "a magnificent diamond of elongated cushion shape and of mixed cutting, weighing 78.54 carats." Archduke Joseph (1872-1962) was a Austro-Hungarian field marshal during World War I. He was the first Regent of Hungary (August-September, 1919) after the fall of the first Hungarian Communist government but was forced to resign, because the Allies would not permit a Hapsburg to hold a commanding position in Hungary.

According to Sotheby's catalog of the jewel sale, it was believed to be the largest unmounted diamond of this quality ever to be offered at auction in Great Britain. It failed to reach its reserve and was withdrawn. The name of the present owner has not been divulged.

Arcots

HE *Arcots,* two well-matched pear-shaped diamonds that weigh a total of 57.35 carats, were first recorded as having been given to Queen Charlotte of England in 1777 by the Nawab of Azim-ub-duala, ruler of Arcot, India. At that time, this was the name of the capitol and two districts of the Carnatic (a name formerly given to a country on the east coast of British India) in Madras Presidency. The Arcot capitol is famous as the site of the military exploits of Clive of India (later Lord Clive), Gover-

Sovereign's Royal Scepter, containing the world's largest fashioned diamond: *Cullinan I.* 530.20 carats. Published by permission of the Controller of Her Britannic Majesty's Stationery Office. Crown copyright reserved

nor of Madras, in the mid-eighteenth century. Today, Arcot is the name of a town in the district of North Arcot, Madras State, Union of India, situated on the Palar River about sixty-seven miles west of the city of Madras.

The two large gems were one of several tribute gifts of Indian princes to Queen Charlotte. On her death in 1818, she specifically named the *Arcot Diamonds* in her will, directing that they be sold for the benefit of her four remaining daughters.

Purchased by Rundell, Bridge & Co., Crown Jewelers, they were held until the death of Bridge and the sale of the business; then, in 1937, they were offered at auction in London. The Marquess of Westminster bought them for £11,000 and subsequently had them set in earrings for the Duchess.

In 1930, the Parisian jeweler, Lacloche, mounted the *Arcots* in the so-called family headpiece of the Westminsters, together with fourteen hundred twenty-one smaller diamonds and a 32-carat central brilliant-cut diamond.

In June, 1959, the third Duke of Westminster, William Grosvenor, decided to sell the headpiece, including the *Arcots,* at Sotheby's. A Bond Street jeweler predicted that it would bring at least $255,000; however, in one of the largest single-jewel sales at any auction, its ownership was transferred to Harry Winston, New York City gem merchant, for $308,000. The two diamonds are now privately owned in Texas.

Ashberg

SHOWN at the 1949 Amsterdam Diamond Exposition, this 102-carat light-yellow diamond was mounted in a necklace with other diamonds and gemstones. It is said to have been part of the ancient Czarist Russian Crown Jewels that were brought to Sweden after the Bolshevic Revolution in 1917.

In 1959, the diamond was offered for sale by the Bukowskis auction house in Stockholm; however, it failed to reach its reserve and was withdrawn. It was sold later by its owner, Mr. Ashberg, through a dealer to an undisclosed buyer.

Austrian Yellow Brilliant

OLD plates show this to be an oval stone with facets covering the top, more in the style of a rose cut than a brilliant. It is not to be confused with the more famous yellow *Florentine Diamond*. Tradition says that the *Austrian Yellow Brilliant* was in the Crown of the Hapsburgs, which dates back to 1602, and is believed to be the work of the court goldsmith of Rudolph II at Prague. The Crown is on view at the Hofburg in Vienna, but it does not contain a gem of this description. The Crown of the Empresses, however, in paintings that still exist, shows large yellow diamonds. This Crown disappeared at the end of the Monarchy in 1918.

According to officials at the *Kunsthistorisches* Museum in Vienna, where the Austrian Crown Jewels are kept and displayed, there are no records of this stone today.

Baden Solitaire

I N 1918, the Austrian Royal Family took many of the Crown Jewels to Switzerland when they went into exile; among them was a 30-carat diamond called the *Baden Solitaire*. It was mounted in the clasp of a 114-pearl necklace, part of a set of diamond-and-pearl jewelry that belonged to the Hapsburgs. Later, it was thought to have been stolen by a person close to the Family and taken to South America with other gems from this historic collection. There is no record of this stone's whereabouts today.

Black Orloff Diamond. 67.50 carats. Courtesy Charles F. Winson, Inc., New York City

Black Orloff

A CCORDING to legend, the *Black Orloff* is said to have taken its name from the Russian Princess Nadia Vyegin-Orloff, who owned it for a time during the mid-eighteenth century. It is a 67.50-carat cushion-cut stone, a so-called black diamond (actually, a very dark gun-metal color). It is reported to have belonged to a nineteenth-century shrine near Pondicherry, India, and to have weighed 195 carats in the rough.

The stone has been exhibited widely, including the American Museum of Natural History in 1951, the Wonderful World of Fine Jewelry & Gifts at the 1964 Texas State Fair, Dallas, and the Diamond Pavilion in Johannesburg in 1967.

The *Black Orloff* is owned by Charles F. Winson, New York City gem dealer, who values it at $150,000. It is mounted in a modern diamond-and-platinum necklace. An alternate name is the *Eye of Brahma Diamond*.

Braganza

HEN Brazil was in the possession of Portugal, a 1680-carat stone was found in that South American country that was said to be a diamond. However, it is generally thought to be a topaz, not a diamond. It has been reported to belong to the Portuguese Government, but officials of that country, in a communication to the Gemological Institute of America, refute this belief. Another name for the *Braganza* is the *King of Portugal Diamond*.

Brunswick Blue

AMED for the Duke of Brunswick, who owned it in the nineteenth century, this 13.75-carat blue diamond is thought to have been one of the stones that resulted from the recutting of the 67.50-carat *French Blue Diamond*, which, in turn, resulted from the cutting of the 112.25-carat *Tavernier Blue Diamond.* Although it is said to have been disposed of in the sale of the Duke's effects in Geneva in 1874, it has taken its place among the historically important diamonds that today must be listed as missing.

The Brunswick Blue II, another pear-shaped blue diamond weighing 6½ carats is believed by some experts to have come from the recutting of the *French Blue Diamond* rather than the 13.75-carat *Brunswick Blue.*

Cape

ICTURED in color in the April, 1958, issue of *National Geographic Magazine* is one of the largest and most perfectly formed diamond octahedra in existence: a 167-carat canary-yellow crystal found in the Dutoitspan Mine, Kimberley, South Africa. Owned by the Diamond Corporation, Ltd., it is valued at approximately $42,000.

Charles The Bold

HARLES the Bold (1433-77) is supposed to have lost this legendary diamond at the Battle of Granson in the last year of his life. It is described as a pyramid-shaped stone, five-eighths of an inch square at its base, with the apex cut in the form of a four-rayed star in relief, each star coinciding with the middle of each face of the pyramid.

It was said to have been bought by King Henry VIII of England from J. J. Fugger, Nuremberg financier, in 1547. In 1554, it was given by Henry's daughter, Queen Mary Tudor, to her husband, Philip II of Spain. At this time, it was a pendant in a necklace of diamonds, rubies and pearls. There is no clue to the location of this stone today.

Cleveland

HE *Cleveland Diamond* is thought to have been the first large diamond cut in New York City. This 50-carat, one hundred twenty-eight facet cushion-shaped stone was fashioned from a 100-carat crystal by S. Dessau of Maiden Lane in 1884.

The stone was named in honor of Grover Cleveland, who had just been elected the twenty-second president of the United States. Minnie Palmer, musical-comedy star of the 1880's, wore it hidden inside a large flower brooch that parted on touch to reveal the gem. It is not known where this stone is today.

Colenso Diamond. 133 carats. Courtesy British Museum of Natural History

Colenso

N 1887, John Ruskin gave a large diamond crystal to the British Museum of Natural History in honor of his friend, John William Colenso, distinguished mathematician and first bishop of Natal, Union of South Africa. The crystal, described as a fine-quality, 133-

carat yellowish octahedron was stolen from the Museum in 1965 and never recovered.

Cross of Asia

SAID to be a champagne-colored diamond, so cut that a Maltese cross is visible from above the table, this stone weighs 109.26 carats and measures 1⅛ x ⅞ x ⅝ inches. It was last reported to be owned by an unnamed charitable institution, which received it by will from a "prominent American." It has been exhibited in stores for a small admission fee, the proceeds from which have been given to the institution.

Efforts to establish the present location and ownership of the *Cross of Asia* by the Gemological Institute of America have proved unsuccessful.

Crown

SOME of the remarkable diamonds of history have origins on which investigators can only speculate. Such a diamond was a remarkable 84-carat, honey-colored, cushion-antique-cut stone that appeared among the lovely gems and jewels originally belonging to the Russian Imperial Family. Unfortunately, this magnificent collection was dispersed and much of it lost to our records when the Imperial Family met its tragic fate in 1917.

About 1935, the *Crown* came to the United States and was exhibited at De Beers *House of Jewels* at the New York World's Fair during 1939-40. Baumgold Bros., New York

11

City diamond firm, bought the stone with the residue of the De Beers Collection after the Fair closed and mounted it in a necklace. Later, the necklace was broken up and the stone recut to a 52-carat round brilliant. It was valued by Baumgold at $150,000.

The *Crown* was shown in a Texas plaque by the Arthur A. Everts Co. of Dallas, at the *Diamonds USA Awards* show in 1949, and was exhibited at the Everts store as recently as 1953. In 1963, the stone was recut a third time, to 50 carats, still retaining its round brilliant style, and sold to an undisclosed buyer.

Cuban Capitol Diamond. 23 carats. Courtesy Academy of Sciences of the Republic of Cuba

Cuban Capitol

N the marble floor of the Cuban Capitol Building, Havana, is a 23-carat yellow African diamond that is used to mark the point from which distances are measured on highways. Workers on the building subscribed $40,000 to purchase the stone in 1928. It was stolen in 1946 but was later recovered and returned to the Capitol.

Cullinan

ATE one afternoon in 1905, Mr. Frederick Wells, superintendent of the prolific Premier Mine in South Africa, was making a routine inspection trip through the mine when his attention was attracted by something reflecting the last slanting rays of the setting sun. Curious, he stopped for a closer look. He was eighteen feet below the surface of the earth, and the shiny object was on the steep wall of the mine a few feet above him. Mr. Wells quickly scaled the wall and extracted from the blueground what appeared to be a large diamond crystal. At first, he thought he was being fooled by a large piece of glass, but tests proved it to be the largest gem-quality diamond ever discovered: It weighed 3106 carats, or about one and one-third pounds, and measured 2 x 2½ x 4 inches! It was named for Sir Thomas Cullinan, who had opened up the Premier Mine and who was visiting the mine on that eventful day.

The *Cullinan* was not an octahedral crystal (two pyramids joined base to base). The largest plane surface appeared to be a cleavage face (formed as a result of a piece being separated from the whole by splitting parallel to planes of atoms arranged parallel to a possible crystal face). Many diamond experts believe that the huge stone was only a fragment, and that another piece (possibly as large, or even larger) either still exists and awaits discovery or was crushed in the mining process. The latter is very unlikely. The prospect of finding the other portion of the colossal diamond has added zest to the activities of numerous miners and prospectors.

The stone was sold to the Transvaal Government,

DIAMONDS...

Cullinan I in the Sovereign's Royal Scepter. 530.20 carats. Published by permission of the Controller of Her Britannic Majesty's Stationery Office. Crown copyright reserved

Cullinan II in the Imperial State Crown. 317.40 carats. Published by permission of the Controller of Her Britannic Majesty's Stationery Office. Crown copyright reserved

which presented it to King Edward VII on his sixty-sixth birthday, November 9, 1907. It was insured for $1,250,000 when it was sent to England. The King entrusted the cutting of the *Cullinan* to the famous Asscher's Diamond Co. in Amsterdam, which had cut the *Excelsior* and other large gems. The huge diamond was studied for months. On February 10, 1908, Mr. Asscher placed a steel cleaver's blade in a previously prepared V-shaped groove and tapped it once with a heavy steel rod; the blade broke but the diamond remained intact! On the second attempt, however, it fell apart exactly as planned, and an employee at the factory reported that afterwards Mr. Asscher fainted. A second cleavage in the same direction produced three principal sections; these, in turn, were divided into nine major gems, ninety-six smaller brilliants and nine and one-half carats of unpolished pieces.

The nine large stones remain either in the British Crown Jewels or in the personal possession of the Royal Family. These historically celebrated gems and their present mountings are as follows: *Cullinan I*, the largest fashioned diamond in the world, is called the *Great Star of Africa*. It is a seventy-four-facet pear-shaped stone and weighs 530.20 carats. King Edward placed it in the Sovereign's Royal Scepter as part of the Crown Jewels, and it is now on display in the Tower of London.

Cullinan II, the world's second largest cut diamond, is a 317.40-carat sixty-six facet cushion-shaped stone. Mounted in the band of the Imperial State Crown, it is also in the Tower of London as part of the Crown Jewels.

Cullinan III, which is a pear-shaped diamond weighing 94.40 carats, was placed in the finial of Queen Mary's Crown and can be worn with *IV* as a pendant-brooch.

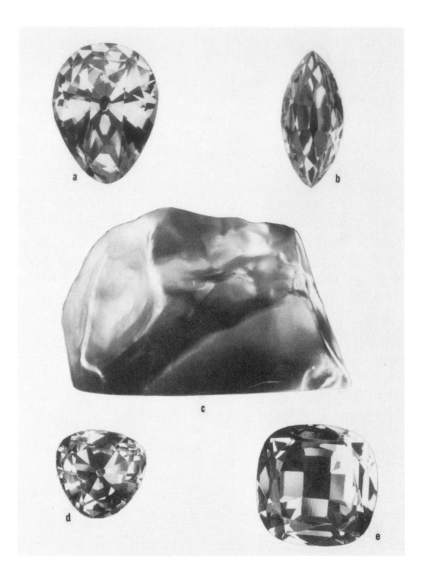

The Cullinan Diamond. (a) Cullinan III, (b) Cullinan VI, (c) Cullinan before cutting, (d) Cullinan V, (e) Cullinan IV (glass replicas). GIA photo not to scale.

Many of Queen Mary's portraits show her wearing these two stones, and Elizabeth II makes use of them in the same way.

The 63.60-carat square brilliant cut, *Cullinan IV,* was set originally in the band of Queen Mary's Crown, but it also can be worn as jewelry, as described above.

Cullinan V, a heart-shaped stone of 18.80 carats, was originally mounted in a brooch for Queen Mary, to be worn alternately in the circlet of her crown as a replacement for the *Koh-i-Noor.* This was after the *Koh-i-Noor* was removed to the new crown that was made for Elizabeth (now the Queen Mother) in 1937.

Cullinan VI, an 11.50-carat marquise-cut stone, was originally presented by King Edward to his wife, Queen Alexandra, and is now worn by Elizabeth II as a drop on a diamond-and-emerald necklace. It is worn more frequently by the young Queen than any other section of the *Cullinan.*

Cullinan VII, an 8.80-carat marquise-cut stone, is mounted as a pendant on a small all-diamond brooch, in the center of which is the 6.80-carat oblong brilliant cut known as *Cullinan VIII.* This brooch also is available for use by the present Queen.

The pear-shaped *Cullinan IX,* a 4.39-carat stone, is mounted in a ring with a carved-claw setting that was made for Queen Mary; it, too, is sometimes worn by Queen Elizabeth.

Cumberland

N appreciation for his victory at the Battle of Cullo-
den in 1746, the City of London purchased a 32-
carat Indian stone for a reported £10,000 and presented it to William Augustus, Duke of Cumberland.
A later Duke of Cumberland, Ernest, the uncle of Queen
Victoria, became King of Hanover, and during her reign
he laid claim to certain jewels. After litigation, these were
restored to the House of Hanover, and some historians say
that the Cumberland was among them.

Darya-i-Nur

ONSIDERED to be the most celebrated diamond
in the Iranian Crown Jewels and one of the oldest
known to man, the 186-carat *Darya-i-Nur* is a
crudely fashioned stone measuring one and one-half
inches long, one inch wide and three-eights of an inch
thick. The name means *Sea of Light, River of Light* or
Ocean of Light.

Both the *Darya-i-Nur* and the historic *Koh-i-Noor* are
said to have been in the possession of the first Mogul emperor of India, from whom they descended to Mohammed
Shah. When the latter was defeated by Persia's Nadir
Shah during the sack of Delhi in 1739, he surrendered all
his chief valuables, including the diamonds and the well-
known Peacock Throne.

After Nadir's assassination in 1741, the *Darya-i-Nur*
was inherited by his grandson, Shah Rokh. Later, it descended in succession to Mirza-Alam Khan Khozeime and

thence to Mohammed Hassan Khan Qajar. Finally, it came into the possession of Lotf-Ali Khan Zand, who was defeated by Aga Mohammed Khan Qajar.

Darya-i-Nur Diamond. 186 carats. Courtesy Central Bank of Iran, Tehran

Imperial State Crown, containing *Cullinan II*. 317.40 carats. Published by permission of the Controller of Her Britannic Majesty's Stationery Office.

In 1797, Aga Mohammed was succeeded by his grandson, Fath Ali Shah, who was both a collector and connoisseur of gems and whose name is engraved on one side of the great diamond.

In 1827, Sir John Malcolm, a British emissary to the Persian Court and author of *Sketches of Persia,* described the *Darya-i-Nur* and the *Taj-e-Mah* (another famous diamond in the Persian Regalia) as the principal stones in a pair of bracelets valued at one million pounds sterling.

During the reign of the next shah, Nasser-ed-Din (1831-96), the stone was mounted in an elaborate frame, which is surmounted by the Lion and Sun (the emblem of the Imperial Government of Iran) and set with four hundred fifty-seven diamonds and four rubies. It is still mounted in the same frame today.

Although some researchers contend that the *Darya-i-Nur* was acquired by the East India Co. and exhibited at London's Crystal Palace Exposition in 1851, Iranian officials at the Central Bank of Iran in Tehran, where the Crown Jewels are kept, told the Gemological Institute of America in 1964 that it has never left the Treasure Vaults.

In 1906, Mohammed Ali Shah, after being defeated by the Constitutionalists while carrying the diamond and other valuables with him during the Persian Revolution, took refuge in the Russian Legation and claimed that the jewels were his personal property. However, as a result of intense efforts made by the freedom fighters, this priceless token of Nadir's conquests was restored to the country.

Today, the *Darya-i-Nur* holds a prominent place among the Iranian Crown Jewels. The Iranian Crown Jewels were studied and authenticated in 1966 by Dr. V. B. Meen of the Royal Ontario Museum. It is now believed that the *Darya-i-Nur* is the major portion of Tavernier's *Great Table.*

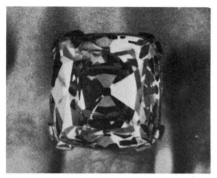

Deepdene Diamond. 104.88
carats

Deepdene

 ANY visitors to the famous Museum of the Philadelphia Academy of Sciences will surely remember
the diamond that was the highpoint of the impressive collection: the 104.88-carat *Deepdene*.

On loan for many years from Cary W. Bok of the
founding family of Curtis Publications, this cushion-cut,
golden-yellow diamond was named after the estate of Mrs.
Bok's family. About 1954, the stone was purchased by
Harry Winston, New York City diamond dealer, who sold
it to an undisclosed buyer. In 1971 a diamond called
Deepdene and weighing 104.52 carats was auctioned at
Christie's in Geneva. Subsequent gemological investigation
proved this diamond to be artificially colored.

Dewey

 HE *Dewey* was one of the first diamond discoveries
in the United States. It was a well-formed but
poor-quality 23.75-carat octahedron that was found
in 1884 by a workman, Benjamin Moore, at Man-
chester, Virginia.

Although Moore placed an arbitrary value of $4000

on the stone, he sold it to Captain Samuel W. Dewey, a geologist and mineralogist, for a reported $1500; he called it the *Or-i-Noor,* or *Sun of Light.*

Dewey Diamond (glass replica). 23.75 carats. Courtesy Smithsonian Institution, Washington, D.C.

After being on exhibition at the New York City jewelry firm of Ball, Black & Co., it was cut into an 11.15-carat stone by Henry D. Morse, a Boston diamond cutter, at an additional cost of $1500. Captain Dewey had glass replicas made of both the rough and the cut stone and sent to the U. S. Mint in Philadelphia, The Peabody Museum of Natural History at Yale University, and the Smithsonian Institution in Washington, D.C.

Eventually, Dewey had to mortgage the diamond and was unable to redeem it. It then became the property of a J. Anglist, who, in turn, mortgaged it for $6000 to John Morrissey, a pugilist, gambler and politician. Since Morrissey's death in 1878, the whereabouts of this stone has been unknown.

Dresden Green Diamond (bottom). 41 carats. Courtesy Historical Museum, Dresden, Germany

Dresden Green

ORTUNATE are those gem lovers who travel to East Germany and have the opportunity to visit the Green Vaults of the State Art Collection in Dresden's Historical Museum. It is here where the unique *Dresden Green Diamond* is on display. The color of the pear-shaped stone is a striking apple green and it weighs 41 carats — the largest historic diamond of this color in existence. It has always been mounted in a shoulder knot, an elaborate pendant-type ornament more than six inches long with two brilliants of about 31 and 13 carats, respectively, and a large number of smaller diamonds.

Although thought to be of Indian origin, the early history of the diamond is unknown, until it appeared at the Leipzig Fair in 1743. There, a Dutch merchant sold it to Frederick Augustus II of Saxony for about $150,000. It then became part of the fabulous Crown Jewels of Saxony, many of which had been collected by Augustus the Strong, father of Frederick, and under whose directions the Green Vaults were constructed.

In 1945, after reposing for more than two hundred years among the Saxon Regalia, the *Dresden Green* was confiscated by the Soviet Trophies' Organization. But it was returned to Dresden in 1958 by the Russians and is again on display in the Museum, where its rare beauty continues to enthrall viewers.

Dresden White Diamond (top). 49.71 carats. Courtesy
Historical Museum, Dresden, Germany

Dresden White

UGUSTUS the Strong of Saxony (1670-1733) was a man of luxurious and extravagant tastes, especially where jewels, paintings and other art objects were concerned. For example, he is reported to have paid between $750,000 and $1,000,000 for a single diamond that struck his fancy: a colorless, square-cut, 49.71-carat stone that came to be known as the *Dresden* (or *Saxon*) *White*. This probably would have been the highest per carat price paid for a diamond at that time.

Like its celebrated companion, the *Dresden Green,* this historically important stone is mounted in an elaborate eighteenth-century shoulder knot (with nineteen other large diamonds and 216 other smaller rose-cut stones) and has long held a prominent place among the Crown Jewels of Saxony in the Green Vaults in Dresden, Germany. It, too, was confiscated by the Russians after World War II but is now back in its familiar resting place in Dresden's Historical Museum.

Dresden Yellow Diamond. 38 carats. Courtesy Historical Museum, Dresden, Germany

Augustus the Strong of Saxony, founder of the Crown Jewels of
Saxony and the Green Vaults, which contain the Dresden Green,
White and Yellow Diamonds

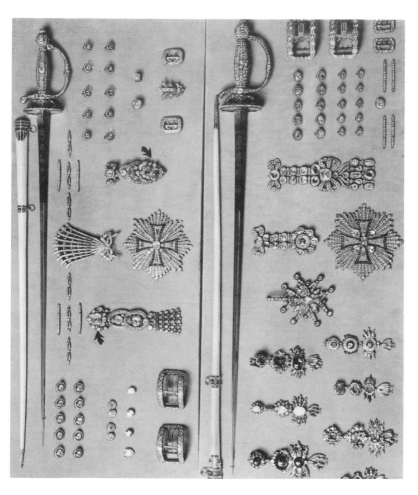

The Diamond Suite in the Green Vaults, Historical Museum, Dresden, Germany. Arrows point to Dresden White (L) and Dresden Green Diamonds (R)

Dresden Yellow

ORMERLY in the famous Green Vaults of the State Art Collection in Dresden, Germany, this 38-carat, yellow, brilliant-cut diamond was confiscated by the Soviet Trophies' Organization in 1945. In 1958, however, it was returned to Dresden by the Russians and is again on display in the Museum.

Dutoitspan Diamond 253.70 carats. Courtesy Smithsonian Institution, Washington, D.C.

Dutoitspan

N 1964, Dutoitspan, the famed mine near Kimberley, South Africa, was the site of discovery of a large, pale-yellow octahedron. It has only a few small black inclusions and is transparent and unusually well formed. It measures about 1½ x 1¼ inches and weighs 253.70 carats.

In the same year, the owner, Harry Winston, New York City gem merchant, donated the superb crystal to the Smithsonian Institution, Washington, D.C., in memory of Sir Ernest Oppenheimer, late Chairman of the Board of DeBeers Consolidated Mines, Ltd. An alternate name is the *Oppenheimer*.

Eagle Diamond. 15.37 carats. Courtesy American Museum of Natural History, New York City

Eagle

HIS 15.37-carat light-yellow diamond, a rounded dodecahedral crystal, was found in 1867 on a farm near Eagle, Waukesha Co., Wisconsin. The discovery was made in hard yellowish earth, at a depth of about forty feet, during a well-digging operation.

The farm wife who sold the stone seven years later to a Milwaukee jeweler for one dollar, thinking it was topaz, sued him when Tiffany's found it was a diamond, for which they had paid the jeweler $850. The crystal was then sold to J. P. Morgan, who later donated it, still uncut, to the permanent collection of the American Museum of Natural History, New York City. In 1965, it was stolen from the Museum, together with other valuable gems, and has not yet been recovered.

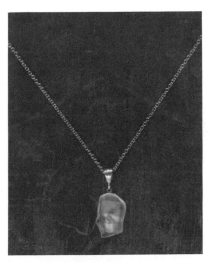

Eisenhower Diamond. 3.11 carats. Courtesy Ruth Larson, Dallas, Texas

Eisenhower

HE "Crater of Diamonds," a kimberlite pipe near Murfreesboro, Arkansas, yielded this 3.11-carat diamond in 1957. The name was chosen by the Dallas, Texas, Gem & Mineral Society, because it resembled the profile of the then President Eisenhower in caricature. In 1958, it was mounted, still uncut, as a pendant with a platinum chain by its discoverer and owner Mrs. Ruth McRae of Irving, Texas, now Mrs. Ruth Larson of Dallas.

Emperor Justinian

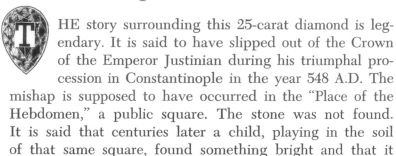

THE story surrounding this 25-carat diamond is legendary. It is said to have slipped out of the Crown of the Emperor Justinian during his triumphal procession in Constantinople in the year 548 A.D. The mishap is supposed to have occurred in the "Place of the Hebdomen," a public square. The stone was not found. It is said that centuries later a child, playing in the soil of that same square, found something bright and that it was the big diamond.

Emperor Maximilian

JUNE 19, 1867, is a date that will be long remembered in Mexican history. On that day, the ill-fated Emperor of Mexico, Ferdinand Maximilian Joseph, was shot to death at Querétaro with his generals, Miguel Miramón and Tomas Mejía. Around his neck at the time of the execution was a little bag containing a diamond that has come to be known as the *Emperor Maximilian*. It is a 42-carat stone with an odd violet fluorescence in daylight. After his death, it was sent to Empress Carlotta, who was then in Europe trying to obtain help for her husband. Later, it was sold to help pay expenses during her mental illness.

The *Emperor Maximilian* was exhibited at the Century of Progress Exposition in Chicago in 1933-34 by its then owner, Ferdinand Hotz, a Chicago diamond dealer. After his death, it was sold to a private collector in New York City, whose name has not been divulged.

Empress Eugenie

ESCRIBED as a perfectly cut, oval-shaped, 51-carat brilliant of unknown origin, the *Eugénie* first came to public attention after Empress Catherine II (Catherine the Great) ascended the Russian Throne in 1762, when she wore it as the center stone in a hair ornament.

About 1787, the Empress presented it to her favorite, Prince Grigori Potemkin, in recognition for his services, both diplomatic and military, and for conducting her triumphant tour through the newly acquired Crimea. She further bestowed on him the surname Taurisschesky (from the name for Crimea, *Khersonesus Taurica*) and a magnificent palace called the *Tauria*. Potemkin died in 1791, after which his extensive collection of jewelry was inherited by his favorite niece, Countess Branitsky, who later willed the stone (then known as the *Potemkin Diamond*) to her daughter, Princess Colorado. From this grandniece of Potemkin, Emperor Napoleon III of France purchased the diamond in 1853 as a wedding gift for his bride, Eugénie de Montijo. Now, mounted in a handsome necklace, Eugénie gave it her own name, by which it is still known today.

After the Franco-German War and the fall of the French Empire in 1870, the Empress escaped to England with some of her jewels, including her beloved diamond, and placed them in safekeeping with the bank of England. Although many of these jewels were sold at Christie's, the renowned London auction house, ownership of the *Eugénie* is said to have been transferred to Mulhar Rao, the Gaekwar of Baroda, for approximately $75,000.

Besides being one of the wealthiest men in the world

Empress Eugénie Diamond. 51 carats

and an avid gem collector, this Maharatta prince became notorious for his reported attempt to murder the British resident, Colonel Phayre, by mixing diamond powder in his food. This was in 1874. But the plot was unsuccessful and he was tried on a charge of poisoning by a jury of three Englishmen and three Indians. The result of the trial was a failure to obtain a unanimous verdict. However, the Viceroy, Lord Northbrook, decided to depose the Gaekwar merely on the grounds of misgovernment! After this incident, the *Eugénie* disappeared, together with many other large diamonds, including the *Star of the South* and the *English Dresden*.

Later (exact date unknown), the *Eugénie* reappeared and came into the possession of Mrs. N. J. Dady of Bombay. Since her death a number of years ago, however, there has been no clue to the present whereabouts of this historically important diamond. All efforts to locate the stone and establish its ownership by the Gemological Institute of America have proved fruitless.

English Dresden

T IS remarkable that two of the finest large diamonds in the world, the *English Dresden* and the *Star of the South*, should have such closely parallel careers. They were found at about the same time, bought in the same city, cut in the same place, handled by the same agency, sent to the same country, and purchased by the same person.

The 119.50-carat *English Dresden* was discovered in the Bagagem Mines, Minas Gerais, Brazil, in 1857. It was thought to be only a portion of a much larger crystal. Taken to Rio de Janeiro, where it was purchased (price unknown) by agents for E. H. Dresden, an English merchant, it was sent to London. Dresden entrusted the cutting to the highly respected Coster plant in Amsterdam. After being fashioned to a well-proportioned 76.50-carat pear shape, it proved to be a flawless, colorless gem.

Comments made at the time on the stone's quality are indicative of the high regard in which it was held. Mr. Dresden himself said, "There is no diamond known in the world today to come up to it. I compared the stone with the celebrated *Koh-i-Noor* at Garrard's one day and, to the surprise of all present, the latter's color seemed yellowish, proof of how perfectly white my diamond must be." A competent appraiser also wrote, "It is perfectly pure, free from defects, and has extraordinary fire and brilliancy. Indeed, the quality of the stone is superior to that of the *Koh-i-Noor*. Yet, when half a share in this magnificent jewel was offered to a noted London jeweller for the relatively small sum of £12,000, he declined it."

First called the *Dresden Drop* and later abbreviated to

Great Chrysanthemum Diamond. 104.15 carats. Courtesy Julius Cohen, Inc., New York City

Dresden, the word *English* was added later, to distinguish it from the *Dresden Green* and other historic diamonds of the same name in the Crown Jewels of Saxony.

English Dresden Diamond
(glass replica). 76.50 carats.
Photo GIA

After being offered to numerous European rulers and other affluent persons, the great diamond was shown to an unnamed Indian rajah, who, although enamored by its scintillating beauty, could not afford the asking price of £40,000. A short time later, in 1864, it was sold to a wealthy English merchant in Bombay; as a result of the cotton shortage caused by the Civil War in the United States, he had made a sudden and unexpected fortune. However, the merchant's agent, who had been sent to Mr. Dresden to consumate the transaction, apparently was not a man of impeccable integrity: He persuaded the owner to accept a lower figure (£32,000) and told the cotton dealer that the original £40,000 asking price had been paid without question, thus enriching his purse with a quick profit of £8000! Although the merchant was now the proud possessor of "the dearest wish of his heart," he was not to enjoy the sparkling loveliness of the diamond for long, for he died a short time later.

In disposing of his estate, the executors were fortunate in being able to recover the $40,000 by selling the now-famous *English Dresden* to Mulhar Rao, the Gaekwar of Baroda, who owned it for an indeterminate number of years. More recently, it is said to have become the property of an Indian, Cursetjee Fardoonji, although it has been impossible to establish this conclusively by direct verification from the owner.

Eureka

HE *Eureka* has the singular distinction of being the first diamond found in South Africa; its name, therefore, is most appropriate. A small boy, Erasmus Jacobs, the son of a Boer widow, picked up some pretty stones in 1866 on the banks of the Orange River and carried them home to his sister, Louisa. She used them to play a game called "five stones." A neighboring farmer, Schalk van Niekerk, was attracted by one of the "pebbles" and asked the widow if she would sell it. She laughed and told him to keep it. He eventually entrusted the 21.25-carat stone to a traveling trader, John O'Reilly, who showed it to Lorenzo Boyes, Civil Commissioner of the town of Colesburg. Later, he took it to Grahamstown, where Dr. W. G. Atherstone, a geologist, identified it as a diamond worth £500. Sir Philip Wodehouse, Governor of Cape Province, purchased the gem at this price. It was shown at the Paris Exposition of 1867-68 and attracted attention to South Africa in general and to the Cape in particular.

In its cut form (a 10.73-carat brilliant), the *Eureka* was owned for many years by an Englishman, Peter Locan. It is known as the *O'Reilly Diamond* in South Africa. This historically important stone was exhibited in 1959 at the Ageless Diamond Exhibition in London. DeBeers Consolidated Mines purchased the stone and presented it to the Parliament of South Africa in Capetown in 1966.

Excelsior

 ROM 1893, when it was found, until 1905 and the discovery of the colossal *Cullinan,* the *Excelsior* was the largest diamond known to man: It weighed 995.20 carats, or about seven ounces!

The Jagersfontein Mine, where it was found, was far from the early river diggings in South Africa; in fact, it was an open-pit mine, where the gems were found in a dry clay miles from any river bed. The huge lump was discovered accidentally by a native, when he picked up a shovelful of gravel he was throwing into a truck. He concealed it from the overseer, until he had an opportunity to deliver it directly to the mine manager. In addition to a cash settlement, he was given a fine horse, a saddle and a bridle.

In shape, the stone was flat on one side and rose to a peak on the other, similar to a loaf of rye bread. This may have suggested the name *Excelsior,* which means *more lofty* or *ever higher.* Its color was said to be a true blue-white, something exceedingly rare in a diamond. Probably, however, it was a typical Jagersfontein product: colorless under incandescent light, but given a bluish cast by the ultraviolet in daylight because of strong fluorescence.

Excelsior Diamond. 995.20 carats

The stone was not cut until 1903, when it was entrusted to the skill of Henry Koe of Asscher's Diamond Co. in Amsterdam. The yield was six pear shapes weighing 69.80, 47.15, 47.03, 34.97, 18.00 and 16.81 carats; four marquise cuts weighing 40.36, 28.55, 26.37 and 24.38 carats; and eleven brilliant cuts, having a combined weight of 20.33 carats. This was a total of 373.75 carats, representing a weight loss of sixty-two and one-half percent. Tiffany & Co. handled some of these stones in its old store on Union Square in New York City, but the exact number and final disposition of each has never been made public. In 1939, one of the marquise cuts was shown by De Beers Consolidated Mines, Ltd., at the *House of Jewels* at the New York World's Fair.

Florentine

NCE the great yellow diamond of the Medici Family, this historic Indian stone is actually light greenish yellow in color and is fashioned in the form of an irregular, nine-sided, one hundred twenty-six-facet double rose cut. It weighs 137.27 carats.

Legends surrounding the stone date as far back as 1467, when Charles the Bold, Duke of Burgundy, is said to have been wearing it when he fell in battle. A peasant or foot soldier found it on the Duke's person and sold it for a *florin*, thinking it was glass, after which it changed hands innumerable times for small sums of money. Pope Julius II is named as one of the owners.

Authentic history begins when Tavernier, the famous French jeweler and traveler, saw the stone among the treasures of the Grand Duke of Tuscany in 1657. When the last of the Medici's died, it passed to Vienna through the marriage of Francis Stephan of Lorraine (who later became the Grand Duke of Tuscany) to Empress Maria Theresa and was placed in the Hapsburg Crown. Later, it was displayed in a brooch among the Austrian Crown Jewels in the Hofburg, Vienna; at that time, it was valued at $750,000.

After the fall of the Austrian Empire, during World War I, the *Florentine* was taken by the Imperial Family into exile in Switzerland. Later, it was thought to have been stolen by a person close to the Family and taken to South America with other gems from the Crown Jewels. After this, it was rumored that the great diamond was brought into the United States in the 1920's and was recut and sold. As a matter of record, it must be listed with other

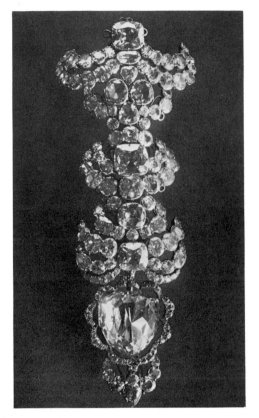

Florentine Diamond. 137.27 carats. Courtesy Museum of Fine Arts. Vienna, Austria

"lost" renowned diamonds of the world. Officials at the *Kunsthistorisches* Museum in Vienna, where the *Florentine* was on display prior to 1918 in a hat ornament, stated to the Gemological Institute of America in 1964 that they have no knowledge of the stone's present location.

Alternate names are the *Tuscan*, the *Grand Duke of Tuscany*, the *Austrian Diamond* and the *Austrian Yellow Brilliant*.

Frankfurt Solitaire

N 1764, Francis I, Grand Duke of Tuscany, purchased a fine-quality brilliant-cut diamond, weighing approximately 45 carats, and had it mounted in his hat buckle. The lovely brilliant came to be known as the *Frankfurt Solitaire*. After the death of Francis, the Empress Maria Theresa had all of her late consort's private jewelry placed in the Royal Treasury for safekeeping; later, however, the stone was brought out and set in a diamond tiara.

In 1918, the Austrian Royal Family took many of the Crown Jewels to Switzerland when they went into exile; among them was the *Frankfurt Solitaire*. About 1920, it was thought to have been stolen by a person close to the Family and taken to South America with other gems from this historic collection. Today, the location of this stone is unknown.

French Blue

HE *French Blue* is a 67.50-carat diamond that is thought to have resulted from the cutting of the 112.25-carat *Tavernier Blue*. Tavernier, the noted French jeweler and traveler, brought the latter to France from India in 1642. He sold the stone to Louis XIV and Pitau, diamond cutter to the King, recut it to a 67.50-carat drop shape. It was in the French Treasury until the great gem robbery of 1792.

Because of its peculiar blue color, some gem historians believe that it was perhaps recut again, producing the world-famous *Hope* and the *Brunswick Blue;* however, their combined weights are too close to that of the *French Blue* to make this plausible.

Garry Moore Diamond. 6.43 carats

Garry Moore

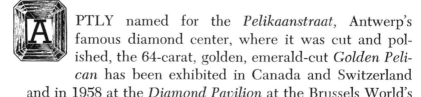

FTER Niels Bach of Ludington, Michigan, discovered this stone in 1960 at the "Crater of Diamonds" near Murfreesboro, Arkansas, he named it in honor of the well-known radio and television personality Garry Moore, because Moore had decided to visit the mine after having Howard Millar, owner of the diamond-bearing property, as a guest on his television program. The diamond is a yellow modified trisoctahedron weighing 6.43 carats; it is flawless and only slightly etched. Schenk & Van Haelen, New York City diamond cutters, appraised it at $6,000.

Golden Pelican

PTLY named for the *Pelikaanstraat,* Antwerp's famous diamond center, where it was cut and polished, the 64-carat, golden, emerald-cut *Golden Pelican* has been exhibited in Canada and Switzerland and in 1958 at the *Diamond Pavilion* at the Brussels World's

Golden Pelican Diamond. 64 carats. Courtesy
E. Sevéry-M. Ginsburg, Antwerp, Belgium

Fair by its owners, E. Sévery and M. Ginsburg of Antwerp. It is valued by the owners at $50,000.

Great Chrysanthemum

N THE summer of 1963, a 198.28-carat fancy brown diamond was found in the South African diamond fields. This unusual stone was purchased by Julius Cohen, New York City manufacturing jeweler, under whose direction it was fashioned by the cutting firm of S & M Kaufman into a 104.15-carat pear shape. It has a total of one hundred eighty-nine facets (sixty-seven on the crown, sixty-five on the girdle, and fifty-seven on the pavilion) and measures twenty-five millimeters wide, thirty-nine long, and sixteen and two-tenths deep. It is mounted as the central stone in a yellow-gold necklace of four hundred ten oval and pear-shaped diamonds, the value of which is stated by the owner to be $540,000.

In the rough state, the diamond appeared to be a light honey color; after cutting, however, it proved to be a rich golden brown, with overtones of sienna and burnt orange, the warm colors of the brown chrysanthemum after which the stone is named.

The *Great Chrysanthemum* has been exhibited by several retail jewelers in the United States and was shown as a *Diamonds International Awards* winner in 1965. In the same year, it was displayed at the Rand Easter Festival in Johannesburg, South Africa.

Great Mogul

OUND in India in the middle of the seventeenth Century, the *Great Mogul,* is said to have weighed 787.50 carats in the rough. It was among the treasures of the famous Shah Jehan, builder of the Taj Mahal and owner of the storied 186-carat *Koh-i-Noor.* He ruled a powerful empire just north of Golconda, India, where diamonds were first discovered.

Aurangzeb, the son of Shah Jehan, showed the great gem to the French traveler and gem expert, Tavernier, presumably the only European to see it. Tavernier, who said it resembled "half of an egg, cut through the middle," published a picture of it, from which all known replicas have been made.

The *Great Mogul* was a rose-cut stone and weighed only 280 carats, according to Tavernier's reckoning at the time he saw it. He was told that Hortensio Borgio, a Venetian who cut the stone from the original 787.50-carat

Great Mogul Diamond (glass replica). 280 carats. GIA Photo

crystal, did such a poor job that the Mogul refused to pay him; rather, he fined him ten thousand *rupees,* his entire fortune! The further history of the stone is unknown, but it is believed to have been among the loot carried off by Nadir Shah, the Persian conqueror, after the sack of Delhi in 1739.

Curiously, the description of the celebrated 189.62-carat *Orloff Diamond* resembles closely that of the *Great Mogul,* except in weight, and some experts think it is the same stone and that Tavernier may have miscalculated in translating the Indian *rati* or diamond weight (1.87 grams), into the European standard, the carat.

Green Brilliant

40-carat, green, brilliant-cut diamond, described by a writer in 1882 as having been worn by the King of Saxony (1697-1733) as a button in the plume of his hat. It should not be confused with the *Dresden Green Diamond,* a 41-carat pear-shaped stone.

The *Green Brilliant* was on display in the Green Vaults
of the State Art Collection in Dresden's Historical Museum
for many years but was confiscated by the Soviet Trophies'
Organization in 1945. In 1958, however, it was returned by
the Russians and is again on display in the Museum.

Harlequin Diamond (pear-shaped stone).
22 carats. Courtesy Wurtemberg Landsmuseum, Stuttgart, Germany

Harlequin

N important part of the Wurttemberg Crown Jewels,
the 22-carat Harlequin Diamond was originally set
in a Golden Fleece for Duke Karl Alexander (1733-
1773). It is now set as a pendant in a three-row,
ninety-seven-stone diamond necklace and is on display in
the Wurttemberg *Landsmuseum*, Stuttgart, Germany.

Hope

T HE 44.50-carat, dark-blue Indian stone known as the *Hope* is undoubtedly one of the world's most celebrated diamonds, although far from being the largest. Past investigators have concluded that a similarity of color between the *Hope* and the 13.75-carat *Brunswick Blue Diamond* provided almost conclusive proof that the two stones were the result of recutting the 67.50-carat *French Blue Diamond*. The *French Blue*, which was stolen from the *Garde Meuble* (Royal Treasury) in 1792 and never recovered, was a drop-shaped stone. Although it is conceivable, and even probable, that the *Hope* was cut from this stone, it is highly unlikely that the *French Blue* could have yielded the *Hope* plus the *Brunswick Blue*.

The *Hope* appeared on the London market in 1830 and was purchased for the gem collection of Henry Philip Hope for $90,000. After Hope's death in 1839, the stone became the possession of his nephew, Henry Thomas Hope, who displayed it at the 1851 Crystal Palace Exposition. By this time, it had acquired its official name.

When the wife of Henry Thomas died in 1887, she bequeathed the now-famous diamond to her youthful grandson, who was her daughter's son and the Duke of Newcastle, if he would agree to adopt the official name of Hope: Henry Francis Hope Pelham-Clinton Hope. This he did, reasoning that the great value of the diamond would more than compensate for the cumbersome name!

In 1894, Lord Hope married Mary Yohe, the American actress. After the marriage, she had a glass model made of the big blue stone for a stage comeback, which proved unsuccessful. Later, in 1906, it was said that Lord Hope

Hope Diamond. 44.50 carats. Courtesy Smithsonian Institution, Washington, D.C.

was in dire financial straits and that he sold the gem in part payment for his debts.

In 1908, Abdul Hamid II, Sultan of Turkey, is reported to have paid $400,000 for it; however, threatened by revolution he returned it to Paris to be resold. Then, in 1911, Pierre Cartier acquired the *Hope* in Paris and sold it for $154,000 to Edward B. McLean, then owner of the *Washington (D.C.) Post*, as a gift for his wife. Mrs. McLean's wealth came from the fabulously rich Camp Bird Mine near Ouray, Colorado. Despite the legends surrounding the *Hope,* including about a dozen violent deaths and disasters to two royal houses, she never considered the stone unlucky, even though her life was plagued by a number of personal misfortunes.

Following Mrs. McLean's death in 1947, Harry Winston, New York City gem merchant, purchased the famous stone for $179,920 and presented it to the Smithsonian Institution in Washington, D.C. In 1962, it was one of the features of the *Ten Centuries of French Jewelry* exhibition at the Louvre Museum, Paris, France.

Hortensia

 LOVELY and unique peach-colored stone of 20 carats that was doubtless worn by Hortense de Beauharnais, Queen of Holland (1783-1837), who was the daughter of Empress Josephine, wife of Louis Bonaparte and mother of Napoleon III.

The catalog of the Apollon Gallery, Louvre Museum, Paris, states that the stone was purchased by Louis XIV and

Hortensia Diamond. 20 carats. Courtesy Archives Photographiques, Paris, France

that later, after the robbery of the Royal Treasury in 1792, it was retrieved from its hiding place under a roof in Les Halles district. It is now on exhibition in the Louvre.

Idol's Eye

AMONG the striking and costly jewels of the late Mrs. May Bonfils Stanton of Denver, Colorado, was a 70.20-carat diamond of fine purity and color known as the *Idol's Eye*. Its history starts in the early part of the seventeenth century, when it was found in India's famed Golconda Mines.

Hope Diamond. 44.50 carats. Courtesy Smithsonian Institution, Washington, D.C.

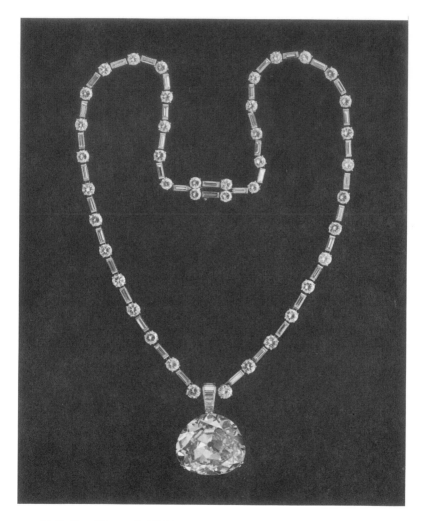

Idol's Eye Diamond. 70.20 carats. Courtesy Parke-Bernet Galleries, Inc., New York City

In 1607, the East India Co. seized the stone from its owner, Persian Prince Rahab, in payment for his debts. It disappeared for three hundred years and was rediscovered in 1906 in the possession of Sultan Abdul Hamid II of Turkey as the eye of a sacred idol in the Temple of Benghazi. After being stolen by the Sultan's messenger and sold to a Paris pawnshop, it was purchased by a Spanish grandee and remained in a safe-deposit vault in London for several years. Later, it was owned by a European diamond dealer.

The *Idol's Eye* was acquired by Harry Winston, New York City gem dealer, who sold it to Mrs. Stanton in 1947 for $675,000. In 1962, it was sold at auction by New York's Parke-Bernet Galleries, Inc., to Harry Levinson, Chicago jeweler, for $375,000. Mr. Levinson exhibited the *Idol's Eye* at the 1967 Diamond Pavilion in Johannesburg. In 1973 Sotheby Parke-Bernet Galleries of New York presented it at auction, but the owner, Mr. Levinson, withdrew the diamond after a disappointing bid of $950,000.

Indore Pears

THESE are two pear-shaped diamonds weighing approximately 50 carats each. Originally from Indore, north-central India, they were once the property of Nancy Anne Miller of Seattle, who, in the 1920's, became the Maharanee of Indore, with much attendant publicity. After her subsequent divorce from the Maharajah, she continued to live in Indore but the diamonds were sold to Harry Winston, New York City gem dealer, and exhibited by him at the *Court of Jewels* at the New York World's Fair in 1949. They are believed to have been sold by Mr. Winston in the mid-1950's.

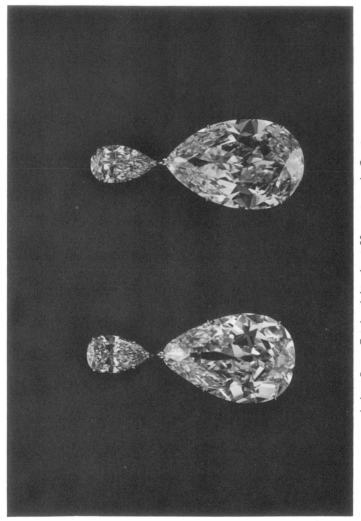

Indore Pears. Total weight: about 50 carats each. Courtesy Harry Winston, Inc., New York City.

Jacob

ONG identified with the Nizam of Hyderabad, the 100-carat *Jacob* was reported to be for sale in 1951, together with a large part of the Nizam's jewels. In 1956, it was held for sale by the Bank of India for $280,000. An American dealer at that time described it as "white, not blue" and not the most brilliant gem he had seen. The present owner of this diamond is not known.

Jagersfontein

HE prolific Jagersfontein Mine in the Orange Free State, South Africa, produced this 215-carat rough in 1889. There seems to be no record of its being cut. The stone's ultimate disposition is unknown.

Jahangir

HE inscriptions on this 83-carat diamond indicate that it was an heirloom of the emperors of the Mogul Dynasty and was probably used to hold the ceremonial plumes on their turbans in place. The Persian engravings show that it first belonged to the Emperor Jahangir and then to his son, Jehan.

In 1954, it was sold in London by its owner, the Maharajah of Burdwan, to Stavros S. Niarchos, Greek shipbuilder and industrialist, for £13,000. In 1957, the *Jahangir* again changed ownership, this time being sold to an Indian businessman, C. Patel, for £14,000, in whose possession it presumably rests today.

Jonker Diamond. 125.65 carats. Courtesy Lazare
Kaplan & Sons, Inc., New York City

Jonker

I N January, 1934, a 726-carat diamond was found on the property of Jacobus Jonker in an alluvial deposit on his farm at Elandsfontein near Pretoria, South Africa. The stone was of unusually fine color and purity. It was purchased by the Diamond Producers' Association for $315,000 and was later sold to Harry Winston, New York City gem dealer, for a reported $700,000.

The diamond was entrusted to Lazare Kaplan, master cutter, who produced a marquise and eleven emerald cuts from it. The Maharajah of Kapurthala bought two of the smaller diamonds for mounting in a ring; the other nine were purchased by private gem collectors. The largest stone, called the *Jonker Diamond*, was a sixty-six-facet emerald cut that weighed 142.90 carats; later, it was recut to 125.65 carats and fifty-eight facets, to give it a more oblong outline.

The *Jonker* was sold to Farouk while he was still King of Egypt. After he went into exile in 1952, the location of the stone became a mystery. In 1959, however, there were rumors that Queen Ratna of Nepal was wearing it, and it has since been confirmed that the late Farouk did sell the great diamond to the little country in the Himalayas for a reputed $100,000.

Reportedly, the *Jonker* was sold in Hong Kong to an unknown businessman for $4,000,000 in 1974.

Jubilee

A 245.35-carat, cushion-shaped, brilliant-cut diamond of unsurpassed color, clarity, brilliance and symmetry — a diamond so perfectly proportioned that it can be balanced on its culet, which is less than two millimeters in diameter! Such is the description of the world-renowned *Jubilee Diamond*.

Jubilee Diamond. 245.35 carats. Courtesy Paul-Louis
Weiller, Paris, France

South Africa's famous Jagersfontein Mine produced this celebrated diamond crystal in 1895. It had an irregular shape, somewhat like a flattened octahedron, but without definite crystal faces. It was first known as the *Reitz Diamond,* in honor of President F. W. Reitz of the Orange Free State. The cutting of the stone took place in 1897 (the year of Queen Victoria's Diamond Jubilee, from which the stone derived its name). A 13.34-carat pear shape also was cut from the same crystal, but its ultimate disposition is unknown.

The *Jubilee* was exhibited at the Paris Exposition of 1900, where it received world-wide attention and the high praise of gem experts. Shortly thereafter, it was sold to Sir Dorab Tata, a *Parsi* of Bombay and the founder of the Indian iron-and-steel industry, who owned it until his death. (Note: A *Parsi* is a person of Persian descent, usually an affluent and highly educated citizen of Bombay City and State, who is an adherent of the ancient Persian religion called *Zoroastrianism.*) In 1939, the executors of Tata's estate sold the stone through Cartier, Ltd., London, to Paul-Louis Weiller, a wealthy and well-known patron of the arts. Weiller lent the *Jubilee* in 1960 to the Smithsonian Institution, Washington, D.C., for an exhibit. In 1966 it was shown at the DeBeers Diamond Pavilion in Johannesburg.

June Briolette

HE *June Briolette* is a pale, greenish-yellow, 48.42-carat briolette-cut diamond. It is suspended in a pin formed of a wreath of oval, round and pear-shaped diamonds of matching colors. Created and owned by Julius Cohen, New York City manufacturing jeweler, the jewel is valued by him at $140,000. (Note: A briolette is a pear-, or drop-shaped, stone with a circular cross section, entirely covered with triangular facets. This form of cutting is very rarely encountered.)

Khedive

N 1869, Ismail Pasha, Khedive of Egypt, presented this 43-carat champagne-colored diamond to France's Empress Eugénie, in honor of the opening of the Suez Canal. It was later owned by King Alphonso of Spain, whose wife was the godchild of the Spanish-born

Empress. The King is said to have sold the diamond in 1930; its reputed value at that time was $500,000. Another owner was Jack M. Werst, Miami, Florida, gem dealer. In the early 1950's, it was reported in the hands of a Ghent dealer, but its present location and owner are unknown.

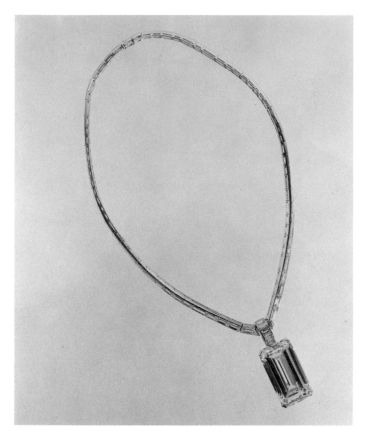

Kimberley Diamond. 55.09 carats. Courtesy Baumgold Bros., Inc., New York City

Kimberley

 HE *Kimberley Diamond* is a flawless, 70-carat, emerald-cut, champagne-colored diamond that was found in the Kimberley Mine, South Africa. It was recut in this modern shape in 1921 from a large, flat stone that was once in the Russian Crown Jewels.

In 1958, the stone was again recut by its owners, Baumgold Bros., New York City, to improve the proportions and increase its brilliancy. It now weighs 55.09 carats and was valued by the firm at $500,000. Baumgold Bros. sold the stone in 1971 to an undisclosed collector.

Koh-i-Noor

HE known facts about the *Koh-i-Noor* date back to the year 1304, when it was owned by the rajah of the huge territory in India known as Malwa, which today is divided into Indore, Ghopal and Gwalior. Two centuries later, it fell into the hands of Sultan Baber, the first of the Mogul emperors. Through his son, it passed down the line to all the great Moguls, including Shah Jehan, who built the Taj Mahal as a memorial for his beloved Queen, Mumtaz. During this period, there was a belief that "he who owns the *Koh-i-Noor* rules the world."

In 1739, Persia's Nadir Shah invaded India, captured Delhi and, after a systematic pillage of the city, seized the diamond. According to one account, the stone was one of the eyes in the peacock in the celebrated Peacock Throne

Koh-i-Noor Diamond (glass replicas).
Before recutting, 186 carats (upper).
After recutting, 108.93 carats (lower).
GIA Photos

Queen Elizabeth the Queen Mother's Crown. Koh-i-Noor Diamond (center), 108.95 carats. Published by permission of the Controller of Her Britannic Majesty's Stationery Office. Crown copyright reserved

that Shah Jehan began and Aurengzeb, his son, completed and that Nadir Shah carried off, thus gaining possession of the jewel.

Another story is that the conquered Mogul ruler, Mohammed Shah, had hidden it inside his turban, which he never removed. When Nadir Shah discovered this, he took advantage of an Oriental custom and invited his victim to a feast, suggesting that they exchange turbans. The vanquished ruler dared not refuse and Nadir Shah, retiring with the turban, unrolled its yards of silk and released the magnificent gem, which fell to the floor. It is then that he is supposed to have cried, "Koh-i-Noor!" (meaning "mountain of light"); thus, the stone was named.

The *Koh-i-Noor* went back to Persia with Nadir Shah but was again in India in the jewel chamber of Lahore, capitol of the Punjab, when that state was annexed to the British Empire. In 1849, the stone was taken by the East India Co. of England as partial indemnity after the Sikh Wars in the Punjab. It was presented to Queen Victoria in 1850 at a great reception in St. James Palace, to mark the two hundred fiftieth anniversary of the founding of the East India Co. by Queen Elizabeth I.

When displayed at the Crystal Palace Exposition in London in 1851, viewers were disappointed that it did not exhibit more fire; therefore, Victoria decided to have it recut. A Mr. Voorsanger, the ablest diamond cutter of Amsterdam's famed Coster plant, came to London for this operation. A four-horse-power steam engine was set up in the workshop of the Crown Jewelers, to drive the wheel. Prince Albert placed the stone on the mill and the Duke of Wellington started the wheel. The cutting required thirty-eight days, which was considered a miracle, since the

Regent had required two years to cut. The operation cost $40,000, and the *Koh-i-Noor* was reduced from its former 186-carat old-Indian cut to a 108.93-carat oval brilliant. Before cutting, it had been valued at $700,000.

Queen Victoria, by the wish of her subjects, wore the big diamond in a brooch; this perhaps gave rise to the superstition that only queens, not kings, could wear it safely. Victoria willed it to her daughter-in-law, Queen Alexandra, who wore it at her coronation. A new crown was made for the late Queen Mary in 1911, with the *Koh-i-Noor* as the central ornament. In 1937, it was transferred to Queen Elizabeth the Queen Mother's Crown. Without the royal arches, the Queen Mother continues to wear the circlet of the Crown, containing the *Koh-i-Noor*, on State occasions. It is one of the principal treasures in the British Crown Jewels in the Tower of London.

Kruger

SOUTH AFRICAN statesman and one-time president of the Transvaal, Stephanus Johannes Paulus (Paul) Kruger (1825-1904), was honored when he was presented with a 200-carat alluvial diamond that was given his name. The stone is said to have changed hands frequently and to have belonged successively to several powerful native chiefs. After its last chief-owner had been taken captive, Kruger freed him. In gratitude, the chief sent the diamond to his benefactor as a gift. The whereabouts of this stone is not known today.

Le Grand Condé Diamond (center). 50 carats. Courtesy Photographie Giraudon, Paris, France

Le Grand Conde

T HE *Grand Condé* is one of the most unusual of the world's notable diamonds: a light pink, pear-shaped stone of 50 carats. Agents of Louis XIII are said to have bought the stone in 1643, after which the King presented it to Louis de Bourbon, Prince of Condé, who had distinguished himself as Commander of the French Army in the Thirty Years' War and who became known as the Grand Condé. Until his death in 1686, the Prince was known as an enthusiastic patron of the arts and an ardent admirer of various charming women, one of whom described him as a much more effective and able general than paramour!

The diamond remained in the Condé family until the Duc d'Aumale bequeathed it to the French Government in 1892. Today, it is on display in the *Museé de Condé* in Chantilly, where, according to the terms of the Duc's will, it must always remain. It is also known as the *Condé Diamond*.

Liberator

I N honor of Simon Bolivar, nineteenth-century liberator of Venezuela, who was affectionately called *El Libertador* by his countrymen, this top-quality 155-carat diamond was given the name *Liberator*. It was discovered by three miners in 1942 in the Gran Sabana diamond-bearing region of Venezuela.

Purchased in 1943 by Harry Winston, New York City gem dealer, it was cleaved into two pieces weighing 115 and

Liberator Diamond. Rough: 155 carats. Courtesy Direccion de Minas, Ministerio de Minas Hidrocarburos, Caracas, Venezuela. Cut: 39.80 carats. Courtesy Parke-Bernet Galleries, Inc., New York City

40 carats. These cleavages, in turn, were fashioned into four stones: three emerald cuts of 39.80, 18.12 and 8.93 carats, and a 1.44-carat marquise. Fifty-six percent of the original weight was lost in the cutting process.

Winston used the three smaller stones in an elaborate clip and sold the 39.80-carat stone to Mrs. May Bonfils Stanton, Denver, Colorado, heiress and philanthropist, in 1947. In 1962, he acquired the stone a second time, purchasing it from the New York auction galleries of Parke-Bernet, Inc., from the jewelry estate of Mrs. Stanton for $185,000. The *Liberator* is set in a platinum ring with two tapering diamond baguettes.

Little Sancy

LTHOUGH from the collection of the same Seigneur de Sancy of the French Court, this 34-carat pear-shaped brilliant cut should not be confused with the 55-carat *Sancy Diamond*. The *Little Sancy* was bought by Prince Frederick of Orange in 1647 and passed down to his grandson, who became King Frederick I of Prussia. The gem was then in the Prussian Treasury for

Little Sancy Diamond. 34 carats. Courtesy Royal Prussian House, Bremen, Germany

many years. It was worn on the Crown Necklace by the bride, Princess Mary of Sachen-Altenburg, at her wedding to Prince Albert of Prussia in Berlin in 1881. In 1923, it was inventoried among the Crown Jewels of the Hohenzollerns as a pendant in a twenty-three-diamond necklace.

Today, still mounted as a pendant but of a much simpler design, the *Little Sancy* is one of the prize possessions of the Royal Prussian House in Bremen, Germany. An alternate name is the *Beau Sancy*.

Major Bowes

NCE owned by the famed originator of the radio amateur hour, the *Major Bowes* is a 44.50-carat yellow diamond. He willed it to Cardinal Francis Joseph Spellman of New York, Roman Catholic clergyman and author. Subsequent owners were C. C. Kaufman of New York City and Erwin Wollands of Cleveland, Ohio. In 1958, while in the possession of Jack M. Werst, Miami, Florida, gem dealer, the gem was stolen in an armed robbery and has never been recovered.

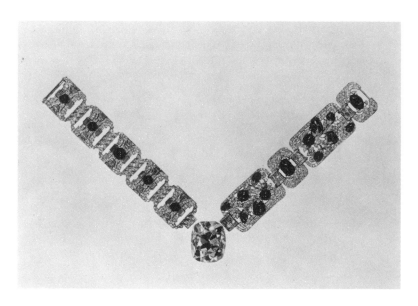

Major Bowes Diamond. 44.50 carats. Courtesy Jack M. Werst, Miami, Florida

Marie Antoinette Necklace. Total weight of diamonds: 2842 carats.
Courtesy N. W. Ayer & Son, Inc., New York City

Marie Antoinette Necklace

ONG associated with Marie Antoinette, Queen of France in the late eighteenth century, this was one of history's most famous pieces of jewelry. The necklace consisted of a total of six hundred forty-seven stones, having a combined weight of two thousand eight hundred forty-two carats. It was made in two sections: a choker with festoons and a large garland for the bodice, which tied at the back of the neck with ribbons. If it were duplicated today with top-quality diamonds, a prominent United States jeweler estimates that the cost would be approximately four million dollars!

In 1785, the necklace was divided and brought to England and sold, and the twenty-two largest stones were incorporated into another neckpiece, now owned by the Duke of Sutherland. In 1959, it was displayed at the *Ageless Diamond Exhibition* in London.

The long, involved history of this notable jewel is documented fully in a book entitled, *The Queen's Necklace*, by Frances Mossiker (Simon & Schuster, New York, 1961).

Matan

HE *Matan* is one of a number of diamonds that is shrouded in secrecy and mystery. A Borneo stone, it is rarely shown and never allowed out of possession of this country's ruler for authentication; therefore, an accurate description is impossible. However, a replica made from heresay depicts the diamond as an unfaceted pear shape.

Matan Diamond (glass replica). 367 carats. GIA Photo

Discovered in 1787, this nearly colorless 367-carat stone is the most notable ever discovered on the Island. It is said to have belonged to the Rajah of Matan, who once was offered $150,000 and two war brigs for it. The stone is thought to have great healing powers and to be a good luck charm. Some investigators believe that it may be rock crystal. Efforts to obtain further information by the Gemological Institute of America were unsuccessful. It is also called the *Rajah of Matan Diamond*. Alternate spellings are *Mattam* and *Matam*.

Maximilian

N 1850, young Archduke Maximilian of Austria purchased a 50-carat greenish-yellow diamond while visiting Brazil and had it cut into a 33-carat cushion cut for his bride, Princess Carlotta of Belgium, who wore it as a pendant. The couple became rulers of

Maximilian Diamond. 33 carats. Courtesy Morris S.
Nelkin, New York City

Mexico and the stone disappeared after Maximilian's execution. In 1901, two Mexicans attempted to smuggle it
into the United States. It was confiscated by the U.S. Government and auctioned off in Customs the same year. A
Congressman Levy is said to have paid $120,000 for it and
to have kept it until 1921, when William R. Phelps, a

jeweler of New York's Maiden Lane, bought the gem for his wife.

In 1946, the stone was acquired by Morris S. Nelkin of New York City. In 1961, suspecting a burglary on the premises, a member of the Nelkin family secreted the pendant, together with other valuables, in a garbage pail and it was inadvertently discarded with the refuse. Since that time, all efforts to recover the diamond have been unsuccessful. It is also called the *Carlotta Diamond.*

Mirror of Portugal

AMES I of England, writing to his son the Prince of Wales, who later became Charles I, mentioned the "Mirroure of Portugall Dyamont," then apparently owned by him. Later, during the Civil War, Charles' wife, Queen Henrietta Maria, is said to have taken the gem to France and to have pledged it with the Duke of Epernon. Cardinal Mazarin is said to have paid off the Duke with the Queen's consent and to have taken possession of the diamond.

The stone is believed to have later been known as the *10th-Mazarin* or the *Mazarin.* Bequeathed by the Cardinal, together with other fine diamonds, to Louis XIV, it became part of the French Regalia, which was stolen from the *Garde Meuble* (Royal Treasury) during the great jewel robbery of 1792. (Note: Cardinal Jules Mazarin (1602-1661) was a French cardinal and statesman and prime minister under Louis XIV. He is given the credit, if not for developing the earliest form of the brilliant, at least for popularizing it.)

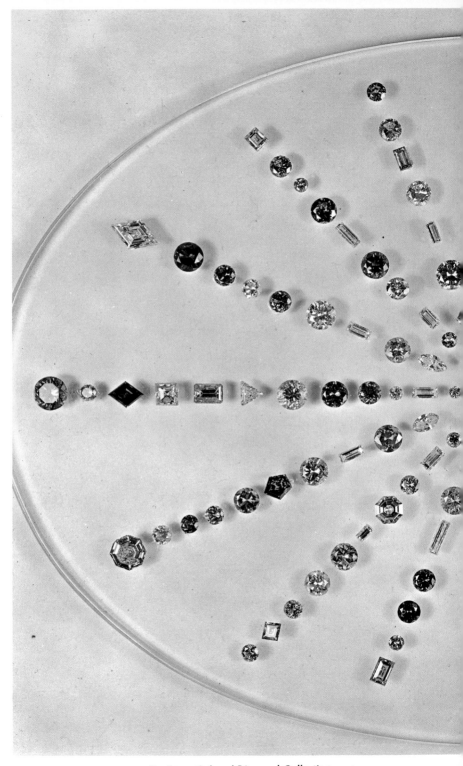

De Beers Colored-Diamond Collection

Moon

A DIAMOND identified by this name, weighing 183 carats, was sold at auction in 1942 to an H. W. Thorne for the low figure of £5200, then passed into the hands of a foreign potentate, whose name was not divulged. The *Moon* was described as a well-cut brilliant, almost circular, rather thick, but with good fire and a faint tinge of yellow. It was one and one-fourth inches in diameter and had a forty-one-facet crown, the bezel facets being divided into two parts.

Almost certainly not Indian in origin, it is more probably South African, which would account for its lack of history. Further details are unavailable.

Moon of Baroda

THE *Moon of Baroda* is said to have been in the family of the Gaekwar of Baroda for about five hundred years. It is a 24.95-carat, pear-shaped, canary-yellow Indian diamond. It was sent to the Empress Maria Theresa of Austria in 1787 by the then Gaekwar, but was later returned to him.

The stone was exhibited in Los Angeles in 1926, and in 1944 the then Gaekwar sold it to Meyer Rosenbaum, Detroit jeweler, for a sum reported to be about $100,000. If it crosses water, it is said to be unlucky for its owner.

Moon of Baroda Diamond. 24.95 carats. Courtesy Meyer
Jewelry Co., Detroit, Michigan

Moon of the Mountains

LTHOUGH the *Moon of the Mountains* was known
to be among the Russian Crown Jewels in the
nineteenth century, today it is considered to be
another celebrated "lost" diamond of history. The
description of this 126-carat Indian diamond by early

chroniclers may have been faulty. Some present-day investigators believe that it may have been confused with
the *Great Mogul, Orloff* and *Darya-i-Nur,* all of which
may refer to the same stone that was taken from Delhi by
the Persian conqueror Nadir Shah and eventually given
to Catherine the Great by Prince Orloff.

Nassak

A S FIRST known in India, the *Nassak* was a 90-carat
triangular-shaped stone; at present it is a magnificent, colorless, 43.38-carat emerald cut. This world-
renowned diamond was once among the treasures
of a Hindu temple near the city of Nassak, where it is said
to have been the eye of an idol of the god Shiva, deity
of destruction and reproduction. After the Maharatta War
of 1818, it fell into the hands of the Marquis of Hastings
and became part of the "Deccan Booty." The great diamond then became known as the *Nassak.*

It was sent to England and was valued at $150,000,
but in 1831 it was sold at auction during a serious de-
pression at the "distress" price of $36,000. In 1837, it again
went to the auction block and was sold to the 1st Marquis
of Westminster, who mounted it in the hilt of his dress
sword.

The stone remained in the Westminster family for
almost a century. Then, it was sold by the 2nd Duke of
Westminster to Georges Mauboussin, the Paris jeweler,
who brought it to America in 1926 for display as an artistic
antique. By this time, it had been cut from its original
Indian weight to an 80.59-carat stone of unusual beauty,
still retaining its triangular shape.

DIAMONDS . . .

Nassak Diamond. 43.38 carats. Courtesy Mrs. William B. Leeds, New York City

The diamond was then returned to Paris, where it was purchased by Harry Winston, New York City gem dealer. Winston brought it back to New York, refashioned it to its present 43.38-carat emerald shape, and sold it to the New York jewelry firm of Trabert & Hoeffer.

Although brilliancy is lessened somewhat by an unorthodox but attractive facet arrangement on the pavilion and a slightly milky body texture, the stone qualifies as one of the most impressive of the world's well-known diamonds. In addition to being flawless and absolutely colorless, the polish is superb and the facet symmetry is above reproach.

In 1944, the *Nassak* was purchased by Mrs. William B. Leeds of New York City, who wore it in a ring with two tapered diamond baguettes. In 1970 it was auctioned at Parke-Bernet Galleries, New York, to Mr. Edward Hand for $500,000.

Another name for the diamond is the *Eye of Shiva*. Alternate spellings sometimes used are *Nasik, Nassac, Nassack* and *Nessuck*.

Nepal Diamond. 79.41 carats. Courtesy Harry Winston, Inc., New York City

Nepal

LITTLE is known about the beautiful 79.41-carat *Nepal Diamond*, except that it is thought to have been mined in India's Golconda region and that it was in the possession of Maharajah Bir Shumsher Jung Bahadur Rana of Nepal in the late nineteenth century. In 1901, it passed to his elder son, Gehendra Shumsher, and it continued in the hands of Nepalese royalty until recent years. The stone has been described as striking and lovely in every respect — colorless, flawless and well cut and polished.

Mounted in an elaborate clip-brooch and pictured in the April, 1958, issue of *National Geographic Magazine*, it was then owned by Harry Winston, New York City gem dealer, who valued it at $500,000. It was shown at London's Ageless Diamond Exhibition in 1959 and subsequently sold in 1961 to a private collector.

Niarchos

THE LATE Sir Ernest Oppenheimer (Chairman of De Beers Consolidated Mines, Ltd., the owner of the Premier Mine, where the stone was found), who had the 426.50-carat rough stone in his personal collection for a short time after the discovery in 1954, valued it at $300,000. It was flawless and of exceptionally fine color.

In 1956, it was sold as part of an $8,400,000 parcel to Harry Winston, New York City gem dealer; the next year, he fashioned it into a 128.25-carat pear-shaped brilliant cut

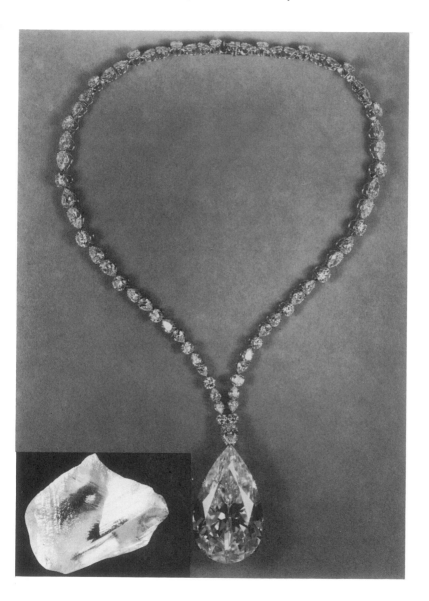

Niarchos Diamond. Rough: 426.50 carats. Cut: 128.25 carats.
Courtesy Harry Winston, Inc., New York City.

with fifty-eight facets on the crown and pavilion and eighty-six additional facets around the girdle. In the same year, it was bought by Stavros S. Niarchos, Greek shipbuilder and industrialist, for a reputed $2,000,000. A 30-carat marquise cut and a 40-carat emerald cut were also obtained from the rough material. It was pictured in color in the April, 1958, issue of *National Geographic Magazine*. Also known as the *Ice Queen*.

Nizam Diamond (glass replica). 277 carats. GIA Photo

Nizam

HE history and description of this large stone is based more on supposition and heresay than on fact. According to the consensus of most gem historians, it was found in Golconda's Kollur Mines about 1835, which is comparatively recent for an Indian diamond, and has been in the possession of the Nizam of Hyderabad since that time.

It is said to have weighed either 340 or 440 carats in the rough state but to have been broken during the Indian Mutiny of 1857. Some investigators state that the broken piece was sold to an Indian banker for 70,000 *rupees*; at that time, its value was placed at £200,000. After cutting, the weight was thought to have been reduced to 277 carats. A glass model (which may or may not be accurate) shows a concave-based, dome-shaped elongated stone, covered with irregular, concave facets.

Much additional conjecture has been written about the *Nizam Diamond*, all of which may pique the imagination but is nevertheless frustrating, confusing and nebulous to the reader and researcher. Presumably, this great diamond has been owned by successive generations of Hyderabad's rulers and retains this status today, although definite confirmation has never been made public knowledge. The name is also sometimes spelled *Nizzam*.

Orchid

D ESCRIBED as having a "pink-lavender color," this 30.45-carat crystal was imported in 1935 by Lazare Kaplan & Sons, Inc., New York City diamond cutters, who fashioned it into a 9.93-carat emerald cut. This rare-colored gem was exhibited in museums in Boston and Cleveland and was sold in 1940 to a private buyer through a wholesaler. One overly poetic gentleman once described it as "containing all the color of a mile of tropical sunset." In 1965 it was reported to have changed hands, but the present owner is unknown.

Orloff

HE 189.62-carat *Orloff* is one of the largest and most historically outstanding diamonds in the world and one of the chief treasures in the Russian Diamond Fund in Moscow. It resembles half of a small egg, is rose cut on top, almost flat and faceted on the bottom, and measures ⅞ x 1¼ x 1⅜ inches.

Stories of the *Orloff's* history differ. Many authorities and writers believe that it is the *Great Mogul*, which was seen in India by Tavernier, the French traveler and jeweler, but that it has been lost to history since that time. If this is true, it was probably part of the 1739 Nadir Shah plunder that was taken during the pillage of Delhi. It is probable that it was stolen after Nadir's assassination and eventually found its way to Amsterdam by devious ways, including theft and murder.

According to another account, the great diamond was originally the eye of the Hindu god Sri-Ranga in a temple in Srirangem, District of Trichonopoly, about one hundred miles from the southern tip of India. It was stolen from the temple by a French soldier, who had deserted the army after fighting in the Carnatic Wars and who fled to Madras and sold the stone to a sea captain for $10,000. The captain, in turn, is said to have sold it in London for $60,000 to a Persian merchant named Khojeh, who took it to Amsterdam. It was there, in 1775, that the Russian nobleman, Count Gregory Orloff, bought the big egg-shaped gem for $450,000 and presented it to Empress Catherine II, in an attempt to regain his place as her favorite. She accepted the gift but refused to reinstate Orloff to his former powerful position in the Court.

Orloff Diamond (glass replica). 189.62 carats.
GIA photo not to scale.

Catherine never wore the *Orloff*, but had it mounted on top of the double eagle in the Imperial Scepter, the form in which it exists today in the Kremlin Museum. The name is also sometimes spelled *Orlov* or *Orlow*. Alternate names sometimes encountered are *Amsterdam*, *Lasarev* or *Septer*.

Pam

AT THE time of its discovery, supposedly sometime before 1891 in the Jagersfontein Mine, South Africa, this diamond weighed between 112 and 115 carats (authorities differ). After being cut into a 56.60-carat brilliant, the *Pam* is said to have attracted the attention of Queen Victoria. She asked to have it shown to her at Osborne House. At that time, the Duke of Clarence, her grandson and heir to the throne, was engaged to marry Princess May of Teck (later Queen Mary). The untimely death of the young Duke in 1892, however, put an abrupt end to the negotiations. The present location of the stone is unknown. An alternate name for it is the *Jagersfontein Brilliant.*

Pasha of Egypt Diamond (glass replica). 40 carats. GIA Photo

Pasha of Egypt

WHEN this diamond was purchased in 1848 by Ibrahim, Pasha of Egypt, for £28,000, it was the most magnificent gem in the Egyptian Treasury; it was described as a 40-carat Indian stone, octagonal in shape and of superior quality. However, when Ismail, the first Khedive of Egypt (1863-1879) was deposed and exiled, historians of the period recorded that he carried with him an immense treasure. Later, it was reported that the diamond had been sold to an unknown Englishman, who subsequently offered it for sale.

The present location and ownership of this stone is uncertain. Possibly, it is still in possession of the Government of the United Arab Republic, but private communications between Cairo officials and the Gemological Institute of America in 1964 failed to offer a definite denial or confirmation of this assumption.

Paul I Diamond. 13.35 carats

Paul I

LIGHT-PINK diamond of fine quality, the 13.35-carat *Paul I* constitutes an important part of the Russian Diamond Fund. Mounted on silver foil, it is the central stone in a diadem of Indian brilliants. The stone was named for Czar Paul, son of Catherine the Great; he is said to have paid 100,000 *rubles* for it.

Peach Blossom

WHEN an inventory was taken of the French Regalia in 1791, the *Peach Blossom* is believed to be the gem that was described as "a pear-shaped diamond of peach-blossom hue, weighing $24^{13}/_{16}$ carats and valued at 200,000 francs." It was purchased by Louis XIV and displayed at the Louvre. The same inventory shows three other smaller stones of the same color, all brilliants, the whereabouts of which is unknown.

Some similarity between this stone and the *Hortensia Diamond* suggests they are the same and perhaps the sole survivor of the peach-colored gems after the theft of the French Crown Jewels in 1792.

Pigott

IT WAS in the year 1818 when Ali Pasha of Janina, ruler of Albania and an enthusiastic gem collector, decided to purchase a large diamond from the London jewelry firm of Rundell & Bridge for $150,-000. Apparently, he was jealous of this newly acquired bauble and kept it in a little green leather bag inside his sash, seldom showing it to others. In 1822, the Sultan of Turkey, overlord of Albania, became resentful of Ali Pasha's mounting power and independence and sent an emissary to demand his surrender. The 80-year-old Pasha was mortally wounded in the palace scuffle that ensued. As he lay dying in his own throne room, he summoned a faithful soldier of fortune, a Captain d'Anglas, and ordered

Pigott Diamond (glass replica). 49 carats. GIA Photo

him to destroy his two most precious possessions: the diamond and his wife, Vasilikee. Although the stone was
shattered before his eyes, he failed to live long enough
to insist on his wife's death and she escaped.

This ill-omened stone, called the *Pigott,* was a fine-
quality, oval-shaped Indian diamond, variously said to have
weighed from 47 to 85.80 carats. Most authorities agree
to 49 carats. It was named for Baron George Pigot (the
correct spelling of the name), twice Governor of Madras,
who was thought to have acquired it as a gift from an
Indian prince in 1763 and willed it to a sister and two
brothers in 1777. Subsequently, it changed hands several
times (once by lottery in 1801) and was said to have been
owned at one time by Madame Bonaparte, mother of
Napoleon.

DIAMONDS...

Since the death of Ali Pasha, there has been no trace of the *Pigott;* likewise, there is no actual evidence of its destruction. Only the model, which had been made previously in England, remains. A less frequently used name is the *Lottery Diamond.*

Pohl

HE 287-carat *Pohl Diamond* was found by Jacobus Jonker, the same man who discovered the famed *Jonker Diamond,* in 1934 in the Elandsfontein diggings near Pretoria, South Africa. The huge, fine-quality stone was cut by Lazare Kaplan for its owner, Harry Winston, New York City gem dealer. The largest finished gem, which was reported sold to an opera singer, was an emerald cut that weighed between 40 and 50 carats. It is also known as the *De Pohl Diamond.*

Polar Star

N LAYMAN'S language, the 41.36-carat *Polar Star* has been described as the "brightest" diamond ever seen — a stone of incomparable beauty and luster. Very little is known of its background, although it is thought to be of Indian origin. It is said to have belonged to Joseph Bonaparte, eldest brother of Napoleon I, who reputedly paid $10,000 for it. Joseph was King of Naples from 1806 to 1808, King of Spain from 1808 to 1813, and lived in the United States from 1815 to 1841.

In the 1820's, the *Polar Star* was sold into Russia. Prince Youssoupoff, who was living in France in 1949, stated at that time that the gem had been owned by his family for more than one hundred years but was later sold to Cartier of Paris. It is now the property of Lady Lydia Deterding, Russian-born former wife of the late oil magnate, Sir Henry Deterding.

The *Polar Star* is presently set in a ring, but detaches to form a pendant.

Polar Star Diamond. 41.36 carats. Courtesy Lady Lydia Deterding, Paris, France.

Porter-Rhodes

CONSIDERED to be the finest African diamond found up to that time (1880), this 153.50-carat stone came from the claim of Mr. Porter-Rhodes in the Kimberley Mine. It was valued at $200,000. In 1881, Mr. Porter-Rhodes visited Osborne House in London and showed it to Queen Victoria, who exclaimed over its great purity and beauty. Empress Eugénie, who also saw the great diamond at the same time, remarked that it was "simply perfection," not knowing what to compare it with. At that time, it was the general belief that South African diamonds were inferior. Victoria asked, "Is it really from the Cape?" Eugénie remarked, "Are you sure the diamond is from South Africa, and have you not had it polished a little? I have always been under the impression that diamonds from the Cape were very yellow and worth but little."

In 1926, the gem was said to have been given as a wedding gift by the Duke of Westminster to his third wife, Loelia Ponsonby; at that time, it was an old-mine-cut diamond of 73 carats. In 1928, it came into the possession of the London jewelry firm of Jerwood & Ward, who had it recut in Amsterdam to a 56.60-carat emerald cut. In 1937, it was reported to have been sold to an East Indian. No additional information is available.

Portuguese

ORMERLY a cushion cut of 150 carats, the *Portuguese Diamond* is today a 127-carat emerald cut and is on permanent display at the Smithsonian Institution, Washington, D.C. It was presented to the Museum in the early 1960's by Harry Winston, New York City diamond merchant. The gem is fluorescent and flawless. The name is taken from the Portuguese Royal House, from which it is said to have had an earlier connection.

Portuguese Diamond. 127 carats. Courtesy Smithsonian Institution, Washington, D.C.

Presidente Vargas

WITH a weight of 726.60 carats, the *Presidente Vargas Diamond* qualifies as one of the largest diamonds ever found. It was discovered in 1938 in the San Antonio River, municipality of Coromandel, Minas Gerais, Brazil, by a native prospector and his partner, a farmer. It was named in honor of the then president of that country, Getulio Vargas. The partners sold the stone to a broker for about $56,000 and it changed hands several times, eventually reaching a reported value of $235,000

Presidente Vargas Diamond. 48.26
carats

Harry Winston, New York City gem merchant, bought the stone in 1939 for approximately $600,000. In 1941, Winston had it cut into twenty-nine stones, the important ones of which were all emerald cuts. The largest of these, which weighs 48.26 carats, is known as the *Vargas* or *Presidente Vargas Diamond*. It was owned for a number of years by Mrs. Robert W. Windfohr of Ft. Worth, Texas, but later came back into the possession of Harry Winston. Ownership of the other stones is not known.

Princess Mathilde

ATHILDE was the cousin of Louis Napoleon (later Napoleon III of France) and hostess for him until his marriage to Eugénie de Montijo; this diamond is thought to have been named for her. Mathilde, who was married to Prince Anatole Demidoff of Russia, had magnificent jewels.

Later, the diamond was also said to have belonged to the great collector, Abdul Hamid II, Sultan of Turkey. Still later, in 1933, it was sold to an undisclosed buyer in Paris by the *Monte de Pieté* (National Pawnshop), which described it as "a brilliant of 16.25 carats and of a special shape that closely resembles the hexagonal."

Princie Diamond. 34.64 carats. Courtesy Van Cleef & Arpels, Inc., New York City

Princie

HE *Princie Diamond*, which apparently has no previously recorded history, is thought to have belonged to the Nizam of Hyderabad at one time. It is a pink, cushion-cut stone of 34.64 carats. In 1960, it was sold at auction by Sotheby's to the London branch of Van Cleef & Arpels for $128,000 and sent to their Paris store. In the same year, it was christened the *Princie* at a party in its honor in Paris. Among the guests were the Maharanee of Baroda and her fourteen-year-old son, the prince heir, whose pet family name is "Princie."

The stone is unmounted. Van Cleef's believe it to be one of the largest and finest pink diamonds in the world; it is described by them as "a true collector's gem."

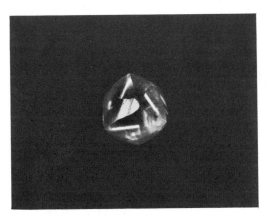

Punch Jones Diamond. 34.46 carats. Courtesy Smithsonian Institution, Washington, D.C.

Punch Jones

NE OF the largest United States diamonds, this 34.46-carat greenish-gray crystal was found in 1928 on Rich Creek near Peterstown, West Virginia. It was discovered by Grover C. Jones and his son, William P. "Punch" Jones, while playing horseshoes but was not positively identified as a diamond until 1943, when it was examined and tested by Professor Roy J. Holden

Famous, Notable and Unique

of Virginia Polytechnic Institute. It is now on permanent display in the Smithsonian Institution, Washington, D.C.

Queen of Belgium Diamond. 40 carats. Courtesy Harry Winston, Inc., New York City.

Queen of Belgium

HIS 40-carat emerald-cut diamond was formerly a 50-carat cushion-shaped stone that belonged to Queen Marie Henrietta of Belgium, wife of King Leopold II. It had been given to her by her mother, the wife of Archduke Joseph, Palatine of Hungary. In its 40-carat version, the *Queen of Belgium* was once handled by Harry Winston, New York City gem dealer, but its present location and owner are not known.

Red Cross

CANARY yellow in color and weighing 375 carats in the rough, this South African diamond was cut into a 205-carat square cut. A "Maltese cross effect" can be seen through the table as a result of cutting. The London Diamond Syndicate presented the stone to the British Red Cross Society and the order of St. John of Jerusalem in 1918. Later in the same year, it was sold to an undisclosed buyer on behalf of the Red Cross at the London auction house of Christie, Manson & Woods for £10,000. For many years it was rumored to have belonged to a royal family in Europe. Sometime prior to 1950, the *Red Cross* was acquired by a Saudi Arabian who sold it in 1973 to an unknown buyer. The stone is now privately owned and deposited in Switzerland where it is presently for sale.

Regent

THE adventurous history of the *Regent* is very much like that of several other great diamonds. Greed, murder and remorse play a part in the opening chapter. Trouble — political, social and personal — accompanies the gem to its last resting place. Originally known as the *Pitt,* this 410-carat stone was one of the last large diamonds to be found in India. It is said to have been discovered by a slave in the Parteal Mines on the Kistna River about 1701. The slave stole the enormous rough stone, concealing it in the bandages of a self-inflicted leg wound, and fled to the seacoast. There, he divulged his secret to an English sea captain, offering him half the value of the stone in return for safe passage to a free country. But during the voyage to Bombay, temptation overcame this seafaring man and he murdered the slave

June Briolette Diamond. 48.42 carats. Courtesy Julius Cohen, Inc., New York City

and took the diamond. After selling it to an Indian diamond merchant named Jamchund for about $5,000, the captain squandered the proceeds in dissipation and, in a fit of remorse and delirium tremens, hanged himself.

Regent Diamond. 140.50 carats. Archives Photographiques, Paris, France

In 1702, Jamchund sold the stone for about $100,000
to Governor Thomas Pitt of Ft. George, Madras, who was
the grandfather of William Pitt of American Revolutionary
fame. Known to historians as the "Elder Pitt," William was
the British Prime Minister for whom Pittsburgh, Pennsyl-
vania, was named. He sent it to England and had it fashioned into a 140.50-carat cushion-shaped brilliant cut,
measuring $1\frac{1}{16}$ x 1 x $\frac{3}{4}$ inches. The cutting took two years
and cost about $25,000, but a number of smaller stones
brought more than $35,000; some of these were rose-cut
stones that were sold to Peter the Great of Russia. The
principal gem, which has but one very small imperfection,
is today considered one of the finest and most brilliant of
the known large diamonds.

In 1717, the gem was sold to Philip II, Duke of Orleans,
then Regent of France, for about $650,000; since that time,
it has been known as the *Regent Diamond*. It was set in the
Crown of Louis XIV and worn at his coronation in 1722.
Removed from the Crown, it was worn by Queen Marie
Leczinska in her hair. Two generations later, when the
French Crown Jewels adorned the Royal Family in many
different kinds of personal ornaments, Marie Antoinette
used the *Regent* to adorn a large black-velvet hat.

This coveted gem disappeared, together with the
equally famous *Sancy* and *French Blue* (from which the
Hope was cut), when the *Garde Meuble* (Royal Treasury)
was robbed of its fabulous jewels in 1792, during the early
part of the Revolution. Some of the gems were soon recovered, but the *Regent* could not at first be traced. After
fifteen months, however, it was found, having been secreted
in a hole under the timberwork of a Paris garret.

In 1797, the great gem was pledged for money that
helped Napoleon in his rise to power. He had it mounted

in the hilt of the sword that he carried at his coronation in 1804. When Napoleon went into exile in Elba in 1814, Marie Louisa, his second wife, carried the *Regent* to the Chateau of Blois. Later, however, her father, Emperor Francis I of Austria, returned it to France and it again became part of the French Crown Jewels.

In 1825, Charles X wore the *Regent* at his coronation; it remained in the Royal Crown until the time of Napoleon III. Then, a place was made for it in a Greek diadem designed for Empress Eugénie.

Many of the French Crown Jewels were sold at auction in 1887, but the *Regent* was reserved from the sale and exhibited at the Louvre among the national treasures. In 1940, when the Germans invaded Paris, it was again sent to the chateau country, this time to Chambord, where it was secreted behind a stone panel. After the War, it was returned to Paris and put on display in the Apollon Gallery of the Louvre Museum. It was one of the features of the *Ten Centuries of French Jewelry* exhibition at the Museum in 1962. An alternate name sometimes used is the *Millionaire Diamond.*

Rovensky Necklace

NE of the most striking and unique diamond-and-platinum necklaces extant, the *Rovensky Necklace* consists of a total of 213.10 carats of diamonds and a colorless, flawless, 46.50-carat pear-shaped pendant as the central stone. The latter gem is from Tiffany & Co. and the others, as well as the setting and metalwork, are by Cartier, Inc.

Rovensky Necklace. Large stone: 46.50 carats. Courtesy Parke-Bernet Galleries, Inc., New York City

This magnificent necklace belonged to the late Mrs. John E. Rovensky of New York City. In 1957, it was sold at auction for $385,000 by Parke-Bernet Galleries, Inc., who stated at the time, "It is the most important item of jewelry ever to be offered at public auction in the United States." The name of its present owner has not been divulged.

Russian Diamond Fund

HE Russian Diamond Fund, also known as the *Russian Treasury of Diamonds & Precious Stones,* is a vast and breathtaking collection of diamond and colored-stone jewelry that comprises the Russian Regalia and the Romanoff Jewels. The diamonds alone weigh a total of more than twenty-five thousand three hundred carats, about fifteen hundred carats of which are represented by seventy important gems, mostly unnamed.

In addition to such world-famous diamonds as the 189.62-carat *Orloff* and the 88.70-carat *Shah* (described elsewhere in the book), a number of the larger, untitled stones weigh from approximately twenty-five to fifty-five carats. Almost all of the fancy colors are represented, including prominent violet, pink and blue. The best-quality stones are of Indian origin, although some good ones are from Brazil and a few from South Africa.

Russian Table Portrait Diamond. About 25 carats

Russian Table Portrait

LSO called the *Russian Tablet Portrait Diamond*, this is a thin flat, irregular pear-shaped diamond that measures 4 x 2.9 centimeters and weighs approximately 25 carats. It belongs to the *Russian Treasury of Diamonds and Precious Stones* in Moscow. Said to be the largest so-called portrait diamond in the world, it is mounted in an old-Indian gold-and-enamel bracelet, Gothic in style. The stone, which is reportedly of fine quality, is thought to be a cleavage from a much larger (Indian) crystal.

Sancy

HE *Sancy Diamond* (full name, *Le Grand Sancy*) has one of the most intriguing and colorful — and certainly one of the most confused and involved — histories of all the famous diamonds of Europe. It is a 55-carat pear-shaped stone, apparently of Indian origin, and is said to be one of the first to be cut with symmetrical facets.

Sancy Diamond. 55 carats. Courtesy the 3rd Viscount Astor, Cliveden, Maidenhead, England

In 1570, the stone was purchased in Constantinople by the French Ambassador to Turkey, Nicholas Harlai, the Seigneur de Sancy, who was an avid collector of gems and jewelry. This passion for personal adornment was more in evidence during the sixteenth and seventeenth centuries in Europe than at any other time or in any other place, except in the East. He brought it to France, where Henry III, who was very sensitive about being bald, borrowed it to decorate a small cap he always wore to conceal his bald pate. Sancy was a prominent figure at the French Court at the time. Henry was the vicious, vain, weak son of Catherine de Medici.

During the next reign, when Sancy was made Superintendent of Finance, Henry IV borrowed the gem as security for a substantial loan to hire soldiers. A messenger was dispatched with the jewel but never reached his destination; thieves had followed him. Knowing that the man was loyal, Sancy made a search for him and his body was discovered, disinterred, and in the stomach of the servant the great diamond was found!

Sancy sold the diamond to James I, and in the 1605 Inventory of Jewels in the Tower of London, the jewel is described in the quaint language of the period: ". . . and one fayre dyamonde, cutt in fawcetts, bought of Sauncy."

It remained in England until 1669. Charles I, son of James I, was beheaded and his widow, Henrietta Maria, presented the jewel to Somerset, the Earl of Worcester, from whom it passed once again to the English Crown. James II later owned it, but he lost all at the disastrous Battle of the Boyne and fled to France. Although Louis XIV was a pleasant and generous host to James, shabby, mournful, exiled kings bored him. James, in desperation, sold the stone to the greedy king, who was known for his love of diamonds. Louis gave him £25,000, which did much to impress James with the security value of gems in time of need!

According to another gem historian, the *Sancy* was sold under different circumstances. During the Civil War, Queen Henrietta Maria took it to the Continent and pledged it, together with other diamonds, to the Duke of Epernon for 460,000 *livres*. In 1657, Cardinal Mazarin paid off the Duke and, with the Queen's consent, took possession of the gems and bequeathed them with other fine stones to Louis XIV.

In 1792, at the beginning of the French Revolution, the *Sancy* and other famous gems were stolen from the *Garde Meuble* (Royal Treasury) in Paris. It reappeared in 1828 and was sold by a French merchant to Prince Anatole Demidoff of Russia; the prince, in turn, is recorded as selling it in 1865 for $100,000. Two years later, it was displayed by the French jeweler, G. Bapst, at the Paris Exposition, bearing a price tag of one million francs.

In 1906, the *Sancy* was purchased by William Waldorf Astor (1st Viscount Astor) as a wedding present when his son (later 2nd Viscount Astor) married Nancy Langhorne of Virginia. Lady Astor often wore the big pear-shaped gem in a tiara on state occasions. In 1962, it was one of the features of the *Ten Centuries of French Jewelry* exhibition at the Louvre Museum. After Lady Astor's death in 1964, the celebrated stone was inherited by her son, the 3rd Viscount Astor. The gem is set in a mounting that permits it to be affixed to the head ornament.

(Note: The Maharajah of Patiala also claims ownership of a "Sancy Diamond." Although this stone also is pear shaped, it weighs 60.40 carats, or about ten percent more than the *Sancy* of the Astor family.)

Searcy

N 1926, while chopping cotton in a field near Searcy Arkansas, a ten-year-old girl named Pellie picked up a "pretty stone." Because of its unusual size, shape and color, she kept it. No one in the community would listen to the little girl when she suggested it might be a diamond. However, after she married a farmer named Howell, she induced him to take the stone to a jewelry store in Searcy. (Searcy is approximately one hundred forty miles from the well-known kimberlite pipe — "The Crater of Diamonds" — near Murfreesboro). The jeweler advised her to send it to the geology department of the University of

Searcy Diamond. 27.21 carats. Courtesy Tiffany & Co., New York City

Arkansas; the University, in turn, suggested showing it to Tiffany & Co. in New York City. In 1946, Mrs. Howell wrote to Tiffany's about the diamond; they later bought it for $8,500.

The *Searcy* weighs 27.21 carats and is described as a well-formed hexoctahedron of fine cape (yellowish) color. Still uncut, it is kept on display at the Tiffany store as the third largest diamond ever found in the United States.

Shah

HE *Shah* is an 88.70-carat, bar-shaped, partially polished diamond bearing three engraved markings. It was probably found in Golconda, India. The first engraving reads, "Bourhan-Nizam-Shah-II, 1000" (Mohammedan calendar), which places the stone in the hands of the ruler of the Indian province of Achmednager in 1591.

The next one reads, "Son of Jehangir Shah — Jehan Shah, 1051." This refers to Shah Jehan, who completed the bejeweled Peacock Throne and built the Taj Mahal (meaning, "Elect of the Palace") for his beloved Queen, Mumtaz Mahal; the date corresponds to 1641.

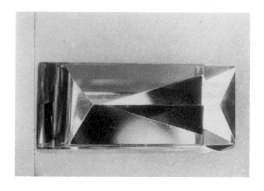

Shah Diamond (glass replica). 88.70 carats.
GIA Photo

He and Mumtaz had a beautiful romance. They met while the Emperor was still young Prince Khurrum. Mumtaz was the daughter of a high-ranking palace official and was of Persian extraction. She had white skin and curling black hair that fell on her shoulders. Persian miniatures show her wearing a flaring crownlike headdress, thickly jeweled, and earrings that fell to her shoulders. She was married to the Prince in 1615 and shared all his campaigns throughout India, meanwhile bearing fourteen children.

Jehan ascended the throne in 1627 and was proclaimed Shah in Agra, near Delhi, the following year. The coronation festivities are said to have cost more than seven million dollars. The Shah was weighed and a like amount of gold, silver and gems distributed to the people. But poor Mumtaz lived only a short time after. She died in 1631 in the Deccan, the region of the great Golconda, while on another expedition with her husband. Jehan then made the construction of the edifice, requiring fourteen years, a major effort of his life.

The *Shah* is believed to be the stone that Tavernier, the French jeweler and traveler, saw dangling before the throne at the Court of Aurungzeb, Jehan's son, in 1665. (Before the completion of Shah Jehan's reign, Aurungzeb rose against his father, imprisoned him and usurped his throne.) How the gem was later carried to Persia is not definitely known; it is possible, however, that Nadir Shah, the Persian conqueror of India, took it in 1739 when he seized the Great Mogul's treasures during the sack of Delhi.

It was during the time that the great diamond was in the possession of the Persian rulers that the third inscription, "Kadjar Fath Ali Shah," who was the Shah of Persia in 1824, was engraved on it. A tiny furrow was also cut on the diamond, possibly to take the cord by which it was suspended.

In 1829, the *Shah* was given to Czar Nicholas I of Russia by the Persian Government in appeasement for the assassination of the Russian Ambassador, Alexander Griboyedoff, in Teheren; thus, it became part of the Crown Jewels of that country.

In 1914, when World War I broke out, the diamond was sent from St. Petersburg to Moscow for safekeeping. After the Revolution, when the strong boxes were opened in 1922 by the new regime, the *Shah* was among the treasures. It is now one of the prize possessions in the *Russian Treasury of Diamonds & Precious Stones* in the Kremlin.

Shah of Persia Diamond. 99.52 carats

Shah of Persia

OT TO be confused with the ancient *Shah Diamond*, the *Shah of Persia* is a 99.52-carat, yellow, cushion-shaped diamond, said to have been part of Nadir Shah's loot after his sack of Delhi in 1739 and to have thus found its way to the Persian Treasury. About the time of World War I, the gem was brought to this country by General V. D. Starosselky, a Russian military expert who had been loaned to Persia by the Czar. It was claimed that the diamond was presented to Starosselky in appreciation for his excellent command of the Persian army.

Mounted in an elaborate pendant-brooch with seventy-two small brilliants and one hundred seventy-eight rose-cut diamonds, the *Shah of Persia* was long owned by Carl D. Lindstrom, Los Angeles gem dealer. In 1957, it was sold to Harry Winston, gem dealer of New York City, who in turn resold it to an undisclosed buyer in 1965.

Sierra Leone I Diamond. 32.12 carats. Courtesy F. J. Cooper, Inc., Philadelphia, Pa.

Sierra Leone I

ROM this 75-carat crystal, found in Sierra Leone in 1959, a magnificent 32.12-carat pear-shaped gem of superb color and clarity was fashioned by Lazare Kaplan & Sons, Inc., New York City diamond cutters. A gem-quality 3.95-carat brilliant cut was also recovered from the rough stone. The 32.12-carat stone was exhibited in Chicago at the *Midwest Trade Show* of the Retail Jewelers of America in 1960. Later, it was owned by the Philadelphia jewelry firm of F. J. Cooper, Inc., but its present ownership has not been made public.

Sierra Leone II

OUND in Sierra Leone in 1959 and cut by Lazare Kaplan, this 115-carat top-quality crystal produced a 15.78-carat marquise-cut stone and two pear shapes, weighing a total of 27.14 carats. These three stones were later offered for sale by the F. J. Cooper firm of Philadelphia, but their final disposition is not known.

Star of Arkansas Diamond. 15.33 carats. Courtesy Arthur A. Everts Co., Dallas, Texas

Star of Arkansas

HE *Star of Arkansas* is one of the largest diamonds ever found in the well-known kimberlite pipe — "The Crater of Diamonds" — near Murfreesboro, Arkansas. The rough stone weighed 15.33 carats and was flawless and colorless. It was elongated and thin, measuring 1½ x ⁷⁄₁₆ x ¼ inches.

The *Star* was cut into a long, narrow, shallow 8.27-carat marquise by Schenk & Van Haelen, New York City diamond cutters, for its discoverer and owner, Mrs. Arthur L. Parker of Taos, New Mexico, and Denver, Colorado.

The value of the finished gem was originallyy established at $11,000 to $15,000; however, its fine quality, uncommonly large size for an Arkansas diamond and attendant publicity led several leading jewelers to reappraise the stone at from $25,000 to $100,000. In 1968 the stone was bought by a Tucson jeweler and resold to a private collector for $50,000.

Star of the East. 100 carats. Courtesy Harry Winston, Inc., New York City

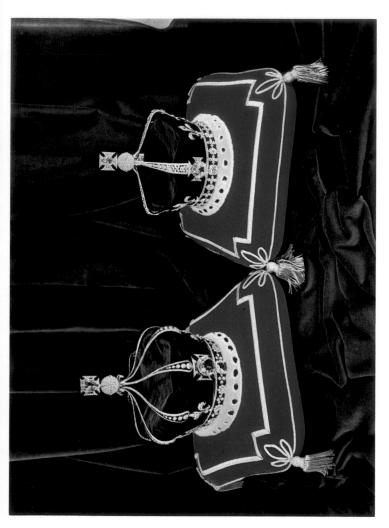

Left: Queen Mary's Crown. Top: Cullinan III. 94.40 carats. Bottom: Cullinan IV. 63.60 carats. Right: Queen Elizabeth the Queen Mother's Crown. Center: Koh-i-Noor Diamond. 108.93 carats. Published by permission of the Controller of Her Britannic Majesty's Stationery Office. Crown copy-right reserved

Star of the East

A 100-carat pear-shaped diamond, believed to be of Indian origin. Abdul Hamid II, Sultan of Turkey, sent the stone to Paris in 1900 to be sold, and in 1908 Mrs. Evelyn Walsh McLean purchased it. She frequently wore the star with the *Hope Diamond,* which she acquired three years later.

In 1949, Harry Winston, New York City gem dealer, bought the *Star* in the jewel estate of Mrs. McLean. It was in the possession of Egypt's King Farouk at the time he went into exile, but had never been paid for.

Star of Este Diamond (glass replica). 26.16 carats. GIA Photo

Star of Este

THE 26.16-carat *Star of Este,* an Indian diamond, was once the proud possession of the Este Family, an ancient ruling house of Lombardy, Italy. The House of Este ruled the Province of Modena in northern Italy from the thirteenth century until Napoleon deposed the last duke in 1796. His daughter, Marie Beatrice, had already married Archduke Ferdinand, one of the sons of Marie Theresa and Emperor Francis I, and the *Star of Este* may have accompanied her to Austria. In the nineteenth century, it was one of the treasures of the Austria-Este Family.

Francis Ferdinand, the last archduke of Austria-Este, whose assassination at Sarajevo precipitated World War I, inherited the diamond; thus, it passed to the Austrian Crown. After his death, it presumably reverted to Emperor Charles but disappeared after he was dethroned in 1919. Reliable reports state that it was sold, together with other jewels, to give financial help to the family of Emperor Carl, who was in exile prior to his death in 1922.

A large diamond of identical description and history was reported to have been purchased by agents of ex-King Farouk of Egypt late in 1950; however, there is no conclusive evidence that this is the same diamond.

Star of Persia

 RESENTLY owned by Harry Winston, the well-known New York City gem dealer, the *Star of Persia* is an 88-carat, yellow, cushion-cut diamond. It is mounted in a modern brooch with one hundred seven baguettes, and the reputed value is $250,000. The gem has been exhibited as the *Good Hope, Spirit of Hope* and *Turkestan,* as well as the *Star of Persia.*

Star of South Africa. 47.75 carats. Courtesy Rudolph Biehler,
Ernest Färber Co., Munich, Germany.

Star of South Africa

HE *Star of South Africa*, a 47.75-carat oval brilliant, cut from a crystal of 83.50 carats, is credited with being the diamond that turned the tides of fortune in South Africa. In 1869, it was picked up by a Griqua shepherd boy on the Zendfontein Farm near the Orange River. Schalk van Niekerk, who two years earlier had had a stroke of luck with a "pebble" that proved to be a 21.25-carat diamond (the *Eureka* or *O'Reilly*), traded the young native for the stone, giving him five hundred sheep, ten oxen and a horse. It was practically all of Niekerk's fortune, but a few days later in Hopetown he sold the rough crystal for $56,000.

Later, the stone was purchased by Louis Hond, a diamond cutter, and fashioned to what is described as an "oval, three-sided brilliant" and was sold to the Earl of Dudley for $125,000. The Countess Dudley wore it as a hair ornament, surrounded by ninety-five smaller diamonds. The present whereabouts of this historically important diamond is not known. It is alternately known as the *Dudley Diamond*.

Star of the South

HE *Star of the South* has the distinction of being the largest diamond (261.88 carats) ever discovered by a woman, as well as the first Brazilian stone to gain worldwide fame. The year of discovery was 1853 and the fortunate woman was a negro slave in the Bagagem Mines of Minas Gerais, who was rewarded with

Star of the South Diamond (glass replica).
128.80 carats. GIA Photo

her freedom and a lifetime pension for finding such an exceptionally large and valuable diamond. Yet, apparently not aware of its true value, her master was induced to sell it for the paltry sum of £3000, after which the purchaser disposed of it in Rio de Janeiro for $30,000!

After changing hands several times, the rough stone was eventually sold for £35,000 and cut at the famed Coster plant in Amsterdam into a 128.80-carat oval brilliant; the cutting cost was $2,500. It was described as colorless, although one observer was quoted as saying that "it had a decided inner-rose tint."

The great diamond was then purchased by a Paris syndicate, christened *Estrella do Sud,* or *Star of the South,* and shown at the 1862 London Exhibition and in Paris five years later, where its size and beauty won international acclaim. At this time, the syndicate was offered £110,000 by an unknown Indian rajah, but the offer was declined. Later, for reasons not divulged, it was sold to Mulhar Rao, the Gaekwar of Baroda, for £80,000, or about $400,000.

The Gaekwar gave the commission for this transaction to E. H. Dresden, who made the original purchase of the well-known *English Dresden Diamond*. In 1934, the potentate's son told Robert M. Shipley, the American gemologist, that both the *Star of the South* and the *English Dresden* were mounted in a necklace among his family's jewels.

In recent years, however, the *Star of the South* has been reported in the possession of Rustomjee Jamsetjee of Bombay, but confirmation has been impossible to obtain by the Gemological Institute of America.

Stewart

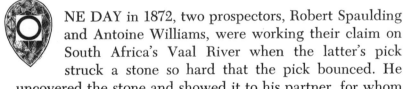 NE DAY in 1872, two prospectors, Robert Spaulding and Antoine Williams, were working their claim on South Africa's Vaal River when the latter's pick struck a stone so hard that the pick bounced. He uncovered the stone and showed it to his partner, for whom it was first named the *Spaulding*. Williams later said he was so excited at the time that he could not eat for two days! The stone, which was slightly yellowish and weighed 296 carats, was for years the largest alluvial diamond ever found. Ironically, their's was a claim that was thought to be outside the best diggings along the Vaal.

The partners sold the crystal for $30,000 to a Port Elizabeth merchant named Stewart, who later sold it for $45,000; the name *Stewart,* however, was retained. The

Stewart Diamond (glass replica). 123 carats.
GIA Photo

stone was eventually cut into a 123-carat brilliant. Its present location is unknown.

Swan

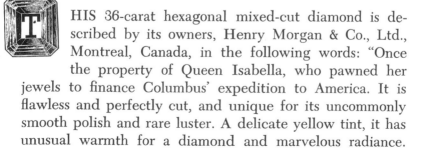

HIS 36-carat hexagonal mixed-cut diamond is described by its owners, Henry Morgan & Co., Ltd., Montreal, Canada, in the following words: "Once the property of Queen Isabella, who pawned her jewels to finance Columbus' expedition to America. It is flawless and perfectly cut, and unique for its uncommonly smooth polish and rare luster. A delicate yellow tint, it has unusual warmth for a diamond and marvelous radiance.

DIAMONDS . . .

Swan Diamond. 36 carats.
Courtesy Henry Birks &
Sons, Ltd., Montreal,
Canada

Throughout its long and exciting history, it has been an important piece in the crown jewels of several European countries, and has been worn by the Queen of Spain, Portugal, Bavaria, Holland, Belgium, France and Austria." The Gemological Institute of America has been unable to verify this description.

Taj-e-Mah

URING the sack of Delhi by the Persian conqueror Nadir Shah, the plunder included not only the *Koh-i-Noor, Darya-i-Nur* and *Akbar Shah Diamonds* but also a 146-carat, rose-cut Indian stone known as the *Taj-e-Mah.* The name means *Crown of the Moon* or

124

Taj-e-Mah Diamond. 146 carats. Courtesy the Central Bank of Iran, Tehran

Crest of the Moon. It is considered a sister stone to the famous *Darya-i-Nur*, and the history of the two follows much the same course.

After Nadir's death in 1747, the *Taj-e-Mah* was rescued from the pillage of his effects and came into possession of his unfortunate successor, Shah Rokh. When this ruler fell into the power of the usurper, Aga Mohammed, he clung desperately to the glittering treasures that had been salvaged from the wreck of his father's property. For many years he endured the cruel treatment and horrible tortures to which Mohammed subjected him. He was exposed alternately to the pains of hunger and thirst and heat and cold, racked and torn with red-hot pincers, and at last deprived of his eyes by the usual Persian method of cold steel. Eventually, his firmness gave way and he relinquished the costly gems one by one.

By these means, Aga Mohammed finally succeeded in acquiring most of the Imperial Crown Jewels, including both the *Taj-e-Mah* and the *Darya-i-Nur*. Soon afterwards, however, he was assassinated by emissaries of a rival faction that was contending for the throne. After his death, the murderers gave all his jewels to Sadek Khan Shekaki, who had been one of his leading generals but who was suspected of having been an accomplice to the murder. Since then, these two renowned diamonds have remained in possession of the Persian monarchs.

Today, the *Taj-e-Mah* occupies an important place among the Crown Jewels of Iran in Tehran. In a communication to the Gemological Institute of America it was described by an authority at the Central Bank of Iran, where the Regalia is kept, as "one of the finest gems in the collection."

Jean Baptiste Tavernier

 FAMOUS French gem dealer and traveler (1605-1689) who made journeys to the East, where he inspected the treasures of many of the potentates and rulers of that time. He described his experiences in a book called *Les Six Voyages of Jean Baptiste Tavernier*, a work to which we owe the descriptions of many of the celebrated diamonds and other gems of the world, both actual and legendary.

Jean Baptiste Tavernier, French jeweler and traveler

Tavernier Blue

HIS is the controversial stone that is thought by some to have produced the 67.50-carat *French Blue Diamond*, which, after being stolen from the French Royal Treasury in 1792, resulted in the 44.50-carat *Hope* and the 13.75-carat *Brunswick Blue*. However, it seems unlikely that a 67.50-carat stone could yield two others with a combined weight of 58.25 carats.

The original weight of the *Tavernier Blue* was 112.25 carats, and it was roughly heart shaped and crudely fashioned. It was bought by this famous French jeweler and traveler in India in 1642 and sold by him to Louis XIV in 1668.

Tiffany

IGHTY years were to pass after its discovery before the 128.51-carat, cushion-cut *Tiffany Diamond* was worn in a piece of jewelry. This is somewhat unusual in itself, but the stone is notable primarily because it is the largest golden-yellow diamond in existence. The 287.42-carat crystal was found in 1887 in South Africa's historic De Beers Mine.

Tiffany's, the famous Fifth Avenue jewelry firm after which the stone is named, bought it the following year and had it cut in Paris under the supervision of Dr. George Frederick Kunz, the company's distinguished gemologist. It has ninety facets: forty on the crown and forty-eight on the pavilion, plus a table and a culet.

Tiffany Diamond (glass replica). 128.51
carats. GIA Photo

More than twenty-five million people are estimated to have seen the great gem in four large expositions: the Chicago Columbian Exposition in 1893, the Pan American Exposition in 1901, the Chicago Century of Progress Exposition in 1933-34, and the New York World's Fair in 1939-40. In the latter, it was outstanding in the fourteen million dollar collection in the *House of Jewels*. The diamond has been on almost continuous display through the years at Tiffany's. One Christmas season it was the feature of the holiday windows, carried by a golden angel and suspended on invisible wires.

The diamond was mounted in a necklace and worn for the first time as a personal ornament at the Tiffany Ball in Newport in 1957. The honor of this first wearing went to the Ball's chairwoman, Mrs. Sheldon Whitehouse.

The value of this outstanding jewel, as estimated by Tiffany's officials, is approximately five million dollars.

Transvaal Diamond. 67.89 carats. Courtesy Baumgold Bros., Inc.,
New York City

Transvaal

HE *Transvaal* is presently a 67.89-carat, champagne-colored, pear-shaped stone. It was cut from a 240-carat crystal that was found in the Transvaal, South Africa. The first cutting produced a 75-carat 116-facet stone that measured 1 x 1⅜ inches; a recutting retained the same length and width but reduced the depth to better proportions, making it more brilliant. The diamond has been featured in several Hollywood films and in leading national exhibitions in the United States and Canada. It is valued by the owner, Baumgold Bros., Inc., New York City diamond firm, at $500,000.

Uncle Sam

HE *Uncle Sam* has the distinction of being the largest diamond ever to be found in North America. It weighed 40.23 carats and was unearthed in Arkansas' "Crater of Diamonds," a kimberlite pipe, in 1924. This fine-quality stone was fashioned into a beautiful 12.42-carat emerald cut by the New York City diamond-cutting firm of Schenk & Van Haelen. It was once sold to a private collector for a price said to be in excess of $50,000. It was owned by Peiken Jewelers, New York City, for many years. Sidney De Young, a Boston dealer, acquired the stone in 1971 and later sold it to a private collector.

Uncle Sam Diamond. 12.42 carats. Courtesy
Peiken Jewelers, New York City.

Venter

THE *Venter* was an enormous, pale-yellow, 511.25-carat alluvial diamond that, at the time of its discovery in 1951, was the largest diamond found in South Africa's Kimberley area until 1974, when an octahedron weighing 616 carats was discovered at the Dutoitspan Mine. The *Venter* was named for the miner, J. Venter, on whose claim it was found.

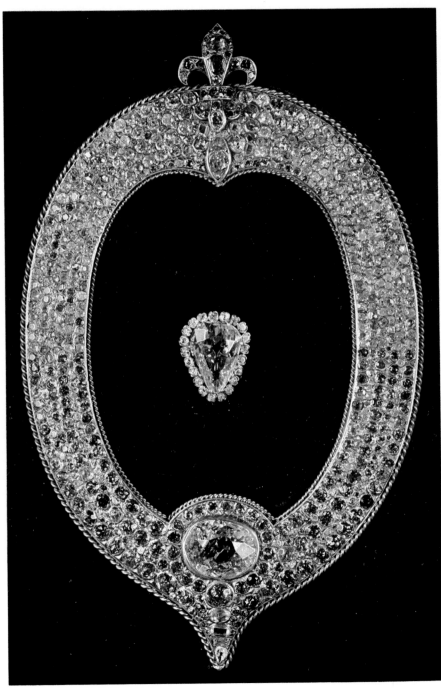

Le Grand Condé Diamond (center). 50 carats. Courtesy Photographie
Giraudon, Paris, France

A well-shaped but badly flawed octahedron, it was cut into thirty-two stones in Johannesburg, the largest of which weighed about 18 carats and the smallest, one-fourth carat.

Victoria

LTERNATE names for this colossal diamond, which weighed 469 carats in the rough, are the *Imperial* or *Great White*. It was found in the Jagersfontein Mine, Orange Free State, in 1884. The Victoria was cut in Amsterdam into a 184.50-carat oval brilliant and a 20-carat round brilliant. The larger stone is thought to have been acquired by the Nizam of Hyderabad for approximately $100,000, but this report has never been confirmed.

Victoria I

WO great diamonds have been given the name *Victoria*. In 1880, a 428.50-carat yellowish stone was discovered in the De Beers Mine, South Africa, and called the *Victoria*; this was four years before the previously described stone appeared in London. This diamond was cut into a brilliant, but reports of its resulting size varied as being either 228.50 or 288.50 carats. It is said to have been sold to an unnamed Indian prince; however, it has been impossible to verify its present ownership.

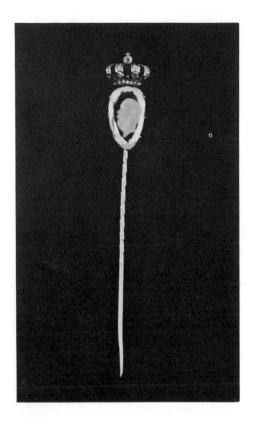

William II of Holland Diamond. 10 carats. Courtesy Chicago Natural History Museum

William II of Holland

 HE intaglio-engraved portrait of William II of Holland on this 10-carat pear-shaped diamond is so delicate that it is necessary to use magnification to appreciate fully the workmanship. It was done by De Vries, a famous diamond cutter of Amsterdam, and is believed to have consumed all his spare time for five years. It is owned by the Chicago Museum of Natural History where it is on display.

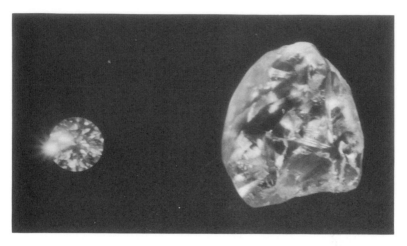

Williamson Diamond. Rough: 54 carats. Cut: 23.60 carats

Williamson

I N 1947, the famous Williamson Mine in Tanganyika was the site of the discovery of one of the most beautiful rose-pink diamonds ever found. Weighing 54 carats in the rough, it was given to Princess Elizabeth on the occasion of her marriage in the same year. The next year, it was cut in London by Briefel & Lemer to a 23.60-carat round brilliant of true rose color. At first, it was thought to be destined for the Royal Crown, but the Queen decided to have it mounted in the center of a brooch designed to resemble an alpine rose with five colorless-diamond petals.

This gem, one of the largest known diamonds of this color known today, has been valued as high as £500,000. In 1959, it was displayed at the *Ageless Diamond Exhibition* in London. It is sometimes referred to as the *Queen Elizabeth Pink Diamond.*

Wittelsbach Diamond. 35.56 carats. Courtesy Christie,
Manson & Woods, London, England.

Wittelsbach

ESCRIBED as a "fine-blue" stone of 35.56 carats, the *Wittelsbach Diamond* was formerly in the Bavarian Crown Jewels, having been brought to the Crown by Maria Amalia of Austria in 1722, during the reign of Maximilian II Emanual of Bavaria. In 1931, the Bavarian Crown Jewels were offered for sale by the London auction firm of Christie, Manson & Woods and the *Wittelsbach* was bid in at £56,000, which was refused. In 1961, it came into the possession of I. Komkommer & Zn., N.V., Antwerp diamond cutter and exporter, who estimated its value at about $750,000. It was loaned by this firm for display by jewelers in both Europe and the United States. Late in 1964, the *Wittelsbach* changed hands once again, this time being sold privately in Germany for an undisclosed sum.

Woyie River

HE 770-carat *Woyie River Diamond* has the distinction of being the second largest alluvial stone ever discovered; it was found in 1945 in the Woyie River, Sierra Leone, Africa. It was a colorless stone and of such clarity that it is not surprising that it was insured for £100,000 while it was being cut in 1953 by Briefel & Lemer of London. Thirty gems were produced, the largest of which weighed 31.35 carats. An alternate name is the *Victory Diamond*.

ABOUT

Other Diamonds

Famous, Notable and Unique

Abadia do Dourados

Found in Minas Gerais, Brazil, mid-1940's. 104 carats. Light brown. Whereabouts unknown.

Abadia do Dourados Lilac

Lilac colored; 63 carats. Found in Minas Gerais, Brazil; date unknown. Sold to an African buyer, 1936, for £10,000. Whereabouts unknown.

Abadia do Dourados Rose

Discovered in Minas Gerais, Brazil; date unknown. 33 carats. Light rose colored. Disposition not known.

Abaeté

Found in Abaeté River, Minas Gerais, Brazil, 1926. Originally owned by Henry Steinberg, Rio de Janeiro jeweler, who later sold it to Fouquet, the Paris jeweler. Location unknown.

Abbas Mîrza

A 130-carat Indian diamond. Thought to have been a cleavage from the larger, more celebrated, *Great Mogul Diamond*. First appeared at the capture of Cûcha in Khurasan by the Persian general Abbas Mîrza in 1832. In 1882, said to have been in Persian (Iranian) Regalia; however, possession denied by Central Bank of Iran in Tehran, where Crown Jewels are kept.

Acaete

Discovered in Brazil, 1791. 161.50 carats. Whereabouts unknown.

Agra

A pink Indian diamond. Thought to have belonged to Baber (1483-1530), first Mogul emperor and great-grandson of Tamerlane, who wore it in his turban. A British officer smuggled it out of Delhi in 1857. Later, owned by Duke of Brunswick. In 1905, sold by Christie, Manson & Wood, the London auction house, for $25,000. Still later, recut in Paris from 46 carats to 31.50 carats, to eliminate imperfections. Subsequent history unavailable.

Ahmedabad

Purchased in India in mid-seventeenth century by Tavernier, the French jeweler and traveler, who had it recut from 157.25 carats to 94.50 carats and disposed of it in Persia (Iran). Present possession has been denied by the Central Bank of Iran in Tehran, where the Crown Jewels are kept.

Amati

Stolen in 1949 from Mrs. N. Coffin, wife of the late short-story writer, Damon Runyon. 31 carats. Maiden name of Mrs. Coffin was Amati. Stone a family heirloom. No further information available.

Antwerp

A large diamond, supposed to have been purchased in Antwerp by King Philip II of Spain as a gift for his third wife, Elizabeth, youngest daughter of Henry II of France. Reportedly weighs 47½ old carats.

Arc

Found on the Vaal River, Cape Province, South Africa, 1921. 381 carats. Whereabouts unknown.

A. Steyn

Found on the Vaal River, Cape Province, South Africa, 1912. 141.25 carats. Disposition unknown.

Banian

Bought by Tavernier, the French jeweler and traveler, in India in the seventeenth century. 48.50 carats. Thought to have been sold to a Dutch sea captain. Additional information unavailable.

Bantam

Described by Tavernier (1648) as a prominent stone in the hilt of a dagger belonging to the Rajah of Bantam. Weight unknown. Whereabouts unknown.

Barkly Breakwater

Found in 1905 at Barkly West, South Africa, during the construction of a breakwater. 109.25 carats. Whereabouts unknown.

Battershill

Discovered at Williamson Diamond Mine, Mwadui, Tanganyika, 1945. Named for Governor of that country, Sir William Battershill. 65 carats. Present location not known.

Baumgold Brilliant

The *Baumgold Brilliant* was originally a round, colorless brilliant of 55 carats, measuring almost one inch in diameter. It was originally cut from a South African rough weighing 167.25 carats. Later, it was recut to a well-made 52-carat stone with a polished girdle before being sold to an undisclosed buyer.

The *Baumgold Rough*, weighing 609 carats, is another diamond found at the Wesselton Mine, South Africa. It should not be confused with the *Baumgold Brilliant*. This was cut into 14 gems in New York City in 1923. The two largest are called the *Baumgold Pears*, weighing 50 carats each.

Bazu

The French jeweler and traveler, Tavernier, obtained this stone in India's Kollur Mines in the seventeenth century. It was sold to a Dutch merchant, who had it cleaved into a number of smaller stones.

Beaumont

Found in the Windsorten area, South Africa; date unknown. 273 carats. Sold to Sir Bernard Oppenheimer, eldest brother of Sir Ernest, for £4000. Sir Ernest (1880-1957) was Chairman of De Beers Consolidated Mines, Ltd. Whereabouts unknown.

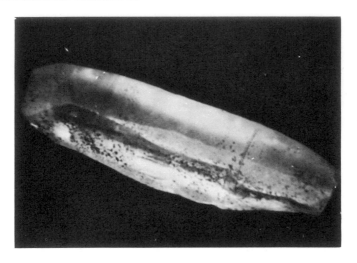

Benedito Valladares Diamond (lead replica). 108.25 carats.
Courtesy Birnbaum Bros., New York City

Benedito Valladares

Discovered in 1940 in the Corrego Coro River, Estrella do Sul, Minas Gerais, Brazil. Purchased by the New York diamond-cutting firm of Birnbaum Bros. and cut into three emerald cuts of 8, 20 and 30 carats. Ultimate disposition of stones unknown.

DIAMONDS . . .

Berglen

One of the largest alluvial diamonds ever found (1924) in South Africa's Transvaal Province. 416.25 carats. Whereabouts unknown.

Birmingham Diamond. 4.25 carats. Courtesy American Museum of Natural History, New York City

Birmingham

Found in 1900 near Birmingham, Shelby Co., Alabama. Unofficial name. Slightly yellow 4.25-carat octahedron. Owned by American Museum of Natural History, New York City.

Black Diamond of Bahia

Discovered in Bahia, Brazil; date unknown. 350-carat black crystal. Shown at 1851 Crystal Palace Exposition in London, where it was described as "so hard it can't be polished." Whereabouts unknown.

Bob Craig

Found in 1917 on the Vaal River, Cape Province, South Africa. 100 carats. Disposition unknown.

Bob Grove

A 337-carat crystal. Found in 1908 on the Vaal River, Cape Province, South Africa. Additional information unavailable.

Brady

Discovered in 1902 on the Vaal River, Cape Province, South Africa. The rough weighed 330 carats. Present whereabouts is unknown.

Brazilia

Flawless and light blue. 176.20 carats. Found on the Abadia do Dourados River, Minas Gerais, Brazil, 1944. Cut in Rio de Janeiro. Ultimate disposition unknown.

Broderick

A 412.50-carat diamond found in 1928 in the Barkly West area, South Africa. Sold to a Mr. F. N. Marcus for about £5000. Present owner unknown.

Burgess

A 220-carat stone. Discovered on the Vaal River, Cape Province, South Africa. Location not known.

Burlington Diamond. 2.11 carats. Courtesy Arthur A. Vierthaler, Madison, Wisconsin

Burlington

Found in 1893 near Burlington, Wisconsin. A 2.11-carat colorless crystal. Owned by Bunde & Upmeyer, Milwaukee jewelers.

Carmo do Paranaiba

Found in the Bededuro River, Minas Gerais, Brazil, 1937. 245 carats. Brown. Disposition unknown.

Carns

Found on the Vaal River, Cape Province, South Africa, 1891. 107 carats. Location unknown.

Cellini Green

"It was green such as you might see in a pale-green emerald, but it shown just like any diamond and as no emerald ever shown." Thus, did Benvenuto Cellini describe this beautiful diamond in his *Treatise on Goldsmithing* (1568), stating further that it was one of the two most beautiful diamonds he had ever seen. Further historical details lacking.

Cellini Peach

Again described by Cellini as one of the two most beautiful diamonds he had ever seen: "A diamond literally flesh colored, most tender, most limpid; it scintillated like a star." Further historical details lacking.

Cent Six

A gem historian in 1882 mentioned this diamond as weighing 106 carats. Its name obviously taken from its weight. Additional details not known.

Chapada

From Chapada district, Minas Gerais, Brazil, 1851. 87.50 carats. No additional information.

Cissie Patterson Necklace

An outstanding diamond necklace, originally owned by the late Mrs. Eleanor Medill Patterson, former owner of the *Washington Times-Herald*. Consists of more than four hundred carats of stones, including a colorless, 22-carat, cushion-shaped center diamond. Owned by Jack M. Werst, Miami, Florida, gem dealer.

Clinch River

Unofficial name. 3 carats. Found in 1889 on Clinch River, Roane Co., Tennessee. Whereabouts not known.

Coromandel I

A 180-carat stone found in Coromandel district, Minas Gerais, Brazil, 1934. Present whereabouts unknown.

Coromandel II

From Coromandel district, Minas Gerais, Brazil, 1945. 141 carats. Ownership not known.

Coromandel III

Found in the Coromandel district, Minas Gerais, Brazil, 1936. 226 carats. Present whereabouts unknown.

Coromandel IV

From Coromandel district, Minas Gerais, Brazil, 1940. 400.65 carats. Disposition not known.

Tiffany Diamond. 128.51 carats. Courtesy Tiffany & Co., New York City

Cruzeiro ou Vitória

A 261-carat diamond found on the San Antonio River, Coromandel district, Minas Gerais, Brazil, 1942. Cut in Rio de Janeiro into six stones of unknown size. Present whereabouts unknown.

Cuiaba

From Cuiaba, Minas Gerais, Brazil; date unknown. 60.75 carats. Light rose colored. Disposition unknown.

Dan Campbell

Found on the Vaal River, Cape Province, South Africa, 1916. 192.50 carats. Present location unknown.

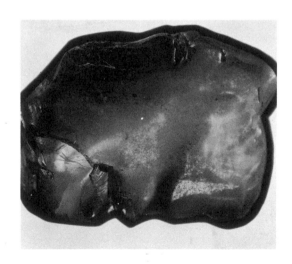

Darcy Vargas Diamond.
460 carats

Darcy Vargas

A 460-carat brown stone found in the Coromandel district, Minas Gerais, Brazil, 1939. Named for the wife of Getulio Vargas, the then Brazilian president. This diamond was displayed at Savitt Jewelers, New Haven, Connecticut, in the early 1940's. Ultimate disposition unknown.

De Beers

A 234.50-carat stone was cut from this 428.5-carat yellow octahedron discovered in the DeBeers Mines, South Africa, in 1888. The diamond was later sold to an Indian prince. Subsequent history and location unknown.

Diário de Minas Gerais

Found in the San Antonio River, Coromandel district, Minas Gerais, Brazil, 1941. 375.10 carats. Present location unknown.

Dowagiac

A 10.87-carat rounded hexoctahedron. Discovered in 1895 near Dowagiac, Cass Co., Michigan. Whereabouts unknown.

Du Toit I

A 250-carat yellowish crystal found in the Dutoitspan Mine, South Africa, 1871. Present ownership unknown.

Du Toit II

A 127-carat yellowish crystal found in the Dutoitspan Mine, South Africa, 1871. Present whereabouts unknown.

Dysortsville

Found in the 1870's near Dysortsville, McDowell Co., North Carolina. A 4.33-carat fine-quality crystal. Owned by American Museum of Natural History, New York City. First owned by Tiffany & Co., who donated it to the Museum's J. Pierpont Morgan gem collection.

Ferdinand

According to a writer in 1882, a 42-carat flawed Indian stone. Found in early seventeenth century and taken to Venice by one Edward Ferdinand for cutting. During early stages of fashioning process, it broke into numerous pieces.

Fineberg-Jones

A fine-quality 206-carat crystal. Found in 1911 on the Vaal River, Cape Province, South Africa. Present whereabouts unknown.

Flower

A 1.95-carat engraved diamond. Owned by Arthur Fine of Max Fine & Sons, Inc., New York City diamond cutters.

Flower Diamond. 1.95 carats. Courtesy Arthur Fine, Max Fine & Sons, Inc., New York City

Gaby Deslys

Given by an unknown Indian maharajah to the late, famous actress for whom it is named. A 28.25-carat, yellow, heart-shaped stone. Later owned by dancer Florence Walton and the "Mystery Chef" of American radio fame. Present owner unknown.

Golconda

In the "Collection of Registered Historic Gems" of Trabert & Hoeffer, Inc., New York City jewelers. A 30-carat emerald cut; fine color and clarity. Their description calls it "one of the last large diamonds from the old Indian mines."

Golden Dawn

Found in 1913 on the Vaal River, Cape Province, South Africa. 133 carats. Cut to a 61.50-carat brilliant. Auctioned

Golconda Diamond. 30 carats.
Courtesy Trabert & Hoeffer, Inc.,
New York City

in 1926 to the Aga Khan for $24,000, in whose family it presumably remains today.

Goyaz

Supposedly, this diamond weighed 600 carats in the rough and one cleavage fragment was cut into an 80-carat stone. Found in 1906 on the Verissimo River, Goyaz, Brazil. Additional data unavailable.

Great Harry

Allegedly, a large (size unrecorded) lozenge-shaped diamond. Part of the Scottish Crown Jewels that James VI

took with him when he became James I of England. At
that time (about 1605), he had it mounted with other gems
in a jewel known as the *Mirror of Great Britain*. Further
information unavailable.

Great Table

A legendary stone, supposedly seen by Tavernier in the
seventeenth century. Weighed 242 French carats, or 250
metric carats. Flat and oblong, with one corner broken
off. Also called *White Tavernier Diamond*. See *Darya-i-Nur*
and *Noor-ol-Ayn*.

Harry Young

Discovered in 1913 on the Vaal River, Cape Province,
South Africa. 269.50 carats. Light yellow. Ultimate disposition unknown.

Harvard

A near perfect 82-carat yellow octahedron was once part
of the James A. Garland Collection, Peabody Museum,
Harvard University. It was stolen in 1962 and never
recovered.

Hastings

A political scandal ensued when this 101-carat diamond
was presented to King George III in 1786 by Warren

Harvard Diamond. 82 carats. Courtesy Harvard University,
Cambridge, Mass.

Hastings, Governor General of India, as a gift from the
Nizam of the Deccan. Hastings, already under a cloud
(later impeached) for his inept administration of India,
was accused of trying to bribe the King with the diamond.
Further historical details lacking.

DIAMONDS...

Heart

Tavernier, the French jeweler and traveler, saw this 35-carat heart-shaped brilliant mounted in an ornament in the treasure of Aurangzeb of India. Additional details lacking.

Holland

According to a gem historian in the latter part of the nineteenth century, a 36-carat conical-shaped diamond in the Crown Jewels of the Netherlands. Whereabouts unknown.

Hornby

Thought to have been brought to England from the East Indies by the Honorable William Hornby, Governor of Bombay, in 1775. It was reported by Streeter in 1882 to weigh about 36 carats. One writer of the nineteenth century expressed the belief that it later came into the possession of the Shah of Persia (Iran). Ownership has been denied by the Central Bank of Iran in Tehran, where the Crown Jewels are kept. However, Dr. V. B. Meen reported in 1966 that a 38.18-carat trapezoid-shaped diamond among the Crown Jewels of Iran could be the *Hornby*.

Independencia

Found in 1941 on the Tyuco River, Minas Gerais, Brazil, 106.82 carats. Present location not known.

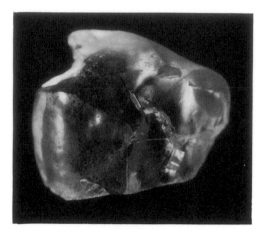

Independencia Diamond. 106.82 carats.
Courtesy Esmeraldino Reis, Rio de Janeiro,
Brazil

Ituiutaba

Found in 1940 in the Ituiutaba Mine, Minas Gerais, Brazil. 105 carats. Disposition unknown.

Jalmeida

A light-yellow stone; 109.50 carats in the rough. Discovered in the Bandeira River, Goyaz, Brazil, 1942. Originally acquired by Steinberg & Byrkett, Rio de Janeiro jewelers. Reportedly cut to 45.40 carats. No additional information.

Joao Neto de Campos

Found on the Paranaíba River, Catalao district, Goyaz, Brazil, 1947. The weight of the rough is reported to be 201 carats. Further details lacking.

DIAMONDS . . .

Julius Pam

From the Jagersfontein Mine, South Africa, 1889. 246
carats; 123 after cutting. Location unknown.

Juscelino Kubitschek

Found in the Estrella do Sul district, Minas Gerais,
Brazil, 1954. 174 carats. Further information not available.

King Charles I Seal

Said to be a carving of the Royal Arms of England.
Weight unknown. Prior to his death in 1649, Charles I
gave the stone to his son Charles II, who needed money
during his exile. The latter is thought to have sold it to
Tavernier, the French jeweler and traveler, who, in turn,
disposed of it in Persia (Iran). Present whereabouts
unknown. In 1966 this diamond was not among the Crown
Jewels of Iran.

Kollur

Bought by Tavernier in 1653 in India's Kollur Mines.
63 carats. Additional details lacking.

La Belle Helene

An exceptionally fine 160-carat alluvial diamond. Found
on the Orange River, South Africa, 1951. Bought by Romi

La Belle Helene Diamond. 160 carats

Goldmuntz of Antwerp for £80,000 and named for his wife. Cut in the U.S. into three stones: two matching pear shapes of 30.28 and 29.71 carats and a 10.50-carat marquise. All were sold privately.

La Favorite

A top-quality 50.28-carat stone. Exhibited at Chicago World's Fair in 1934, when it was owned by a Persian and valued at $1,000,000. Present location unknown.

La Reine des Belges

A 50-carat diamond. Thought to have been owned by Queen of Belgium in latter part of nineteenth century. Existence not verified.

Lee Diamond. 4.50 carats. Courtesy American Museum of Natural History, New York City

Lee

Unofficial name. A 4.50-carat distorted octahedron. Found in Lee Co., Alabama, at turn of century. Owned by American Museum of Natural History, New York City; it was stolen in 1964 and never recovered.

Leopold

A 10-carat brilliant. Given by King Leopold III of Belgium to his late wife, Queen Astrid, mother of present King Baudouin. Exhibited at Newark, New Jersey, Museum, 1948. Owned by undisclosed private collector.

Light of India

A large (weight unknown) diamond that belonged to the late Boston socialite, Mrs. Jack Gardner. Worn as a hair ornament, set on a spring, to wave about the head like an antenna. Owned by another Bostonian; name undisclosed.

Litkie

Found on the Vaal River, Cape Province, South Africa, 1891. 205 carats. Location unknown.

Mahomet IV

A legendary stone. 24 carats. Found in Constantinople on a heap of rubbish by a poor man during reign of Mahomet IV (1648-87). The finder sold the stone for a pittance, but it was later seized by the Grand Vizier and added to Imperial Treasures. It adorned the Imperial Plume of the Sultan of Turkey on parade days. Present-day ownership denied by *Topkapi Muzesi Mudurlugu,* where Turkish Regalia is kept.

Mascarenhas I & II

Seen by Tavernier in Goa in 1648. Belonged to Portuguese Viceroy, Dom Philip Mascarenhas. 57 and 67.50 carats, good quality, Indian cut. Additional information lacking.

Mato Grosso

Found in Mato Grosso, Brazil, 1963. Described as "very deformed, having an undefinable brown-rose-violet color, and showing no inclusions under 5x." Disposition unknown.

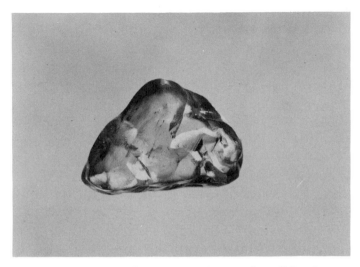

Mato Grosso Diamond. 227 carats. Courtesy Esmeraldino Reis,
Rio de Janeiro, Brazil

McFarlin

A 49.40-carat, emerald-cut canary stone officially known
as the *Myrtle McFarlin Canary Diamond*. It was purchased
in 1956 by the McFarlin family in New York and donated
to the Witte Memorial Museum in San Antonio, Texas, in
1961. In 1968 it was stolen from the museum and never
recovered.

Mendelsohn

Owned by Parliament of Union of South Africa. A
5-carat alluvial stone. Mounted in a man's ring and engraved with the initials "S. M." for its owner, Sidney
Mendelsohn, diamond-field pioneer and philanthropist, who
willed it to Parliament on his death.

Milford

A fine-color diamond; 6 carats. Found near Milford, Clermont Co., Ohio, 1879. Whereabouts unknown.

Minas Gerais

Found on the San Antonio River, Minas Gerais, Brazil, 1937. 172.50 carats. Location unknown.

Mirror of Naples

A fine-quality diamond; size unknown. Belonged to Mary, sister of Henry VIII, who married Louis XII of France. At that time, valued at about 30,000 crowns ($37,500). Further historical details lacking.

Morrow

Largest diamond found in Georgia: a 4.50-carat yellowish crystal. Discovered at Morrow Station, Clayton Co., 1887. Present location not known.

Mountain of Splendor

Allegedly, a 135-carat stone in Persian Regalia. Possession denied by Central Bank of Iran, Tehran, where Crown Jewels are kept.

DIAMONDS ...

Napoleon

A 34-carat brilliant-cut stone. Supposedly, sold to Napoleon Bonaparte for £8000 to decorate his sword on day of his wedding to Josephine. He carried it as a talisman, until lost at Battle of Waterloo. Further details lacking.

Nepal Pink

Reported by a U.S. gem dealer, while in Nepal in 1959, as a 72-carat old-Indian cut with a "soft, rose-pink color." Present ownership unknown.

Noor-ol-Ayn

A 60-carat pink diamond. Set in a diadem with three hundred twenty-three smaller diamonds. Name means *Light of the Eye*. Belongs to Iranian Crown Jewels. Believed to have been cut from the *Great Table*. See *Darya-i-Nur*. Alternate spelling is *Nur-ul-Ain*.

Noor-ud-Deen

A large (size unknown) pink diamond. Belonged to Prince Alexander Tzary in nineteenth century. Name means *Light of Faith*. Mounted in center of a cross, containing eighty-five brilliants and one hundred sixty rose cuts. Sold in London in 1898 for £750. No additional information available.

Nova Estrella do Sul

Means *New Star of the South.* 140 carats; greenish. Found in Abaeté River, Minas Gerais, Brazil, 1937. Present location unknown.

Oregon Diamond. 3.87 carats. Courtesy American Museum of Natural History, New York City

Oregon

A 3.87-carat, grayish-green distorted octahedron. Found in 1893 near Oregon, Dane Co., Wisconsin. Purchased by Tiffany & Co. for $50 and presented to American Museum of Natural History, New York City. It was stolen from the Museum in 1964 and never recovered.

Orpin-Palmer

Found in 1902 on the Vaal River, Cape Province, South Africa. 117.50 carats. Valued at £1000. Whereabouts unknown.

Otto Borgstrom

A well-formed yellowish octahedron; 121.50 carats. Found in the Vaal River, Cape Province, South Africa, 1907. Additional information lacking.

Paolo de Frontin

A slightly greenish, 49.50-carat Brazilian stone. Sold in London in 1936. No other information available.

Patos

Found in the Patos Mine, Minas **Gerais**, Brazil, 1937. 324 carats; brown. Location not known.

Patrocino

Discovered in the Patrocino River, Minas **Gerais**, Brazil, 1851. Disposition not known.

Peace

Found in 1962 in Yakutiya region of Siberia. 56.20 carats. Further details not available.

Pindar

Sir Paul Pindar brought this stone to England from Constantinople and sold it to Charles I. Valued at $150,000.

Thought to have been among the royal jewels on which Henrietta Maria, his wife, raised $10,000 in one year. Subsequent history lost.

Pointe de Bretagne

The great diamond (weight unrecorded) of the French House of Dunois. Set with hanging ruby drops. Francis I, who initiated the Crown Jewels of France as a permanent collection, wore the diamond and drops in his cap. Further information lacking.

Pointe de Milan

A point-cut diamond. Part of the dowry of Catherine de Medici, niece of Pope Clement III, when she married the future King Henry of France in 1533. She gave it to her daughter-in-law, Mary Stuart, afterward Queen of Scotland, who married Francis II of France in 1559. Additional historical details lacking. (Note: The *point cut* was the earliest form of diamond cutting, consisting of merely polishing the natural faces of an octahedron. Also called *diamond point*.)

Pope Paul III

Holy Roman Emperor Charles V presented this stone to Pope Paul III when he entered Rome in 1536. Benvenuto Cellini, in his *Autobiography*, tells of setting the diamond in a ring for the Pope, for which the Emperor paid him 12,000 crowns. Further historical details lacking.

Presidente Dutra Diamond. 409 carats. Courtesy Esmeraldino Reis, Rio de Janeiro, Brazil

Presidente Dutra

Discovered in the Douradinho River, Coromandel district, Minas Gerais, Brazil, 1949. 409 carats. Produced thirty-six stones, totaling one hundred thirty-six carats. The largest weighed 9.60 carats; the smallest, .55 carat. Also called the *Dutra*.

Prince Edward of York

A 60.25-carat pear-shaped stone. Imported to the U.S. in 1901 by Alfred H. Smith & Co. and sold to a New York banker. Ultimate disposition unknown.

Prince Edward of York Diamond. 60.25 carats

Queen Frederica Diamond. 2 carats. Courtesy Max Fine & Sons, Inc., New York City

Queen Frederica

An engraved diamond. It is wafer thin, colorless, weighs slightly less than two carats and measures 7 x 10 millimeters. The gem bears the portrait of Frederica Louisa Wilhelmina, wife of William I, Prince of Orange and the first king of the Netherlands. She was the great-great-grandmother of present Queen Juliana. Owned by Max Fine & Sons, Inc., New York City, since 1920.

Queen of Holland

Described as an "intense blue." A 136.25-carat cushion-shaped stone. Cut in Amsterdam in 1904 and owned there for many years by the firm of F. Friedman. Exhibited at Paris Exposition of Arts & Industry in 1925. Later, sold by a Paris jeweler to an Indian maharajah for an estimated $1,000,000. Present whereabouts unknown.

Queen of Holland Diamond. 136.25 carats. Courtesy
Freeman-Lewis, Inc., New York City

Rajah

A large (weight unknown) diamond that belonged to the late Boston socialite, Mrs. Jack Gardner. Worn as a hair ornament, set on a spring, to wave about the head like an antenna. Owned by another Bostonian; name undisclosed.

Raulconda

Seen by Tavernier at India's Raulconda Mines in mid-seventeenth century. 103 carats. Additional information unavailable.

Regale of France

Historical records state that Louis IX of France disguised himself as a pilgrim and brought this stone (size unknown) as an offering to the Shrine of St. Thomas á Becket in England, receiving in turn a small leaden figure of St. Thomas. Present location unknown.

Regent of Portugal

A Brazilian stone, found in 1775, cut into a 215-carat round brilliant. It is thought to be a topaz, not a diamond. Additional details lacking.

River Styx

A coarse and knotty black crystal. Found in the Bultfontein Mine, South Africa. Purchased from a European

River Styx Diamond. 28.50 carats. Courtesy Jack M. Werst, Miami, Florida

Saukville Diamond. 6.57 carats. Courtesy Arthur Vierthaler, Madison, Wisconsin

dealer by Jack M. Werst, Miami, Florida, gem dealer, and cut to a 28.50-carat brilliant and a 7-carat marquise. The cleaving and polishing, done by New York City diamond cutter Maurice Italiaander, required several months because of the knots. In 1958, stolen in an armed robbery and never recovered.

Rosa de Abaeté

Found in Abaeté River, Minas Gerais, Brazil, 1935. 80.30 carats. No further information available.

Saukville

The finder, Conrad Schafer, owned this 6.57-carat stone fifteen years before learning it was a diamond. Found in 1881, near Saukville, Wisconsin. Owned by Bunde & Upmeyer, Milwaukee jewelers. Uncut.

DIAMONDS...

Savoy

A 54-carat table-cut diamond. Described by Tavernier in the mid-seventeenth century as being among the Crown Jewels of the House of Savoy. Nothing else is known of the stone. (Note: The *table cut* was probably the earliest symmetrical style of fashioning in diamonds. Opposite points of the octahedron were ground down to squares to form a large culet and a larger table; the eight remaining portions of the eight octahedral facets were then polished. Still used for some *calibre-cut* stones; i.e., very small square rectangular, keystone or other shapes set in ring shanks, band rings, bracelets and other similar kinds of jewelry, usually in lines or masses.)

Scorgie

A 21-carat golden-yellow diamond. Found in the Kimberley Mine, South Africa (date unkown). Named for the discoverer, a miner, who refused £825 but later sold it for £500. The buyer, a Scottish military doctor, had it cut in England. Weight after cutting and present owner not known.

Sea of Glory

A 66-carat stone, once believed to be one of the principal gems in the Persian (Iranian) Regalia. In 1966 this diamond was not among the Crown Jewels of Iran. Present whereabouts unknown.

Shepherd Diamond. 18.30 carats.
Courtesy Smithsonian Institution,
Washington, D.C.

Shepherd

A flawless, canary-yellow stone cut in the cushion-brilliant style. 18.30 carats. Owned by the Smithsonian Institution, Washington, D.C.

Southern Cross

Found in 1929 on Abaeté River, Minas **Gerais**, Brazil, near place where Southern Cross Constellation was discovered. A rose-colored stone. 118 carats. Present location unknown.

Stanley

Found in 1900 in a branch of Gold Creek, Morgan Co., Indiana. Greenish yellow. 4.87 carats. Cut into a 1.12- and a 1.06-carat stone.

Star of Beaufort

A South African stone, supposed to have weighed in excess of 100 carats. Nothing else is known.

Star of David

A crystal that bears a perfect outline of the Star of David. Found in the Transvaal, South Africa, 1955. Additional details unavailable.

Star of Diamonds

Said by a nineteenth-century writer to be a 107.50-carat, high-quality South African diamond, found in the early days of the diamond fields. No further information available.

Star of Egypt

Found about 1850 and acquired by the Viceroy of Egypt. A 250-carat oval stone. Appeared later in London as a 106.75-carat emerald cut. Present location and ownership not known.

Star of Minas

Found in the Bagagem Mines, Minas Gerais, Brazil, in 1910. 179.30 carats. Disposition unknown.

Star of Sarawak

A 70-carat Borneo stone. Purchased from a Chinese merchant and miner by the Rajah of Sarawak. Later displayed in London. Additional details unavailable.

Star of Zion

Found on the Vaal River, Cape Province, South Africa, 1917. 85 carats; exceptional color and purity. Sold for £34 a carat. Present whereabouts unknown.

Sultan Baber

A legendary stone. Supposed to have disappeared with the Great Mogul and other gems during Nadir Shah's sack of Delhi in 1739. No other historical details.

Table

Purchased by Francis I of France in 1532 for 65,000 *ecus*. One of the finest and largest then known (size unrecorded). Later, became part of the King's personal treasury. Subsequent history not known.

Tavernier A

An oval-shaped, 51-carat brilliant. One of twenty that Tavernier, the French jeweler and traveler, bought in India and sold to Louis XIV. Stolen in Paris in 1792 from the

Royal Treasury with other gems of the French Regalia. Descriptions of the *Empress Eugénie* and *Tavernier A* are identical, and some historians believe they are the same. Additional details lacking.

Tavernier B

A 32-carat uncut stone, also bought by Tavernier and sold to Louis XIV. Cannot now be identified with any existing gem.

Tavernier C

Another gem that Tavernier sold to Louis XIV. 31 carats. Brilliant cut. Also stolen from the Royal Treasury. Nothing else known.

Tavernier Pear

A 54.75-carat, pear-shaped brilliant. Said to have been seen by Tavernier in India in 1685. Historical records indicate it was among the loot taken by Nadir Shah during his sack of Delhi in 1739. Later, it dropped from sight in Paris.

Tennant

A 112-carat yellowish stone. Given to James Tennant, London mineralogist, in 1873 by one of his students. Later, cut to a flawless 68-carat stone. Whereabouts unknown.

Theresa

Found at Kohlsville, Washington Co., Wisconsin, in 1886. 21.25 carats. In 1918, cut in New York City, producing a total of 9.27 carats; the largest, 1.48 carats. Crystal had dividing line, separating almost colorless from a yellowish section. Ultimate disposition of stones unknown.

Three Tables

Three table-cut diamonds, weighing from 48 to 52 carats. Said to have been seen by Tavernier in India in 1665. Historical records indicate they were carried off by Nadir Shah during his pillage of Delhi in 1739. Other details lacking.

Throne

The 90-carat stone Tavernier saw in India in the seventeenth century and described as one of the ornaments in the fabled Peacock Throne. No other records available.

Tigereye

Found in the Vaal River, Cape Province, South Africa, in 1913. 178.50 carats. Amber colored. Cut to a 61.50-carat brilliant. Ultimate disposition unknown.

Tiros I

Found in the Tiros district, Minas Gerais, Brazil, 1938. 354 carats. Brown. Location not known.

Tiros II

Found in the Tiros district, Minas Gerais, Brazil, 1936. 198 carats. Rose-colored. Location not known.

Tiros III

Found in the Tiros district, Minas Gerais, Brazil, 1936. 182 carats. Colorless. Location not known.

Tiros IV

Found in the Tiros district, Minas Gerais, Brazil, 1938. 173 carats. Brown. Location not known.

Tiros Lilac

Found in the Tiros district, Minas Gerais, Brazil, 1938. Lilac colored. 12.25 carats. Location not known.

Turkey I & II

Two diamonds, 84 and 147 carats, last reported (1882) in the Turkish Regalia. Additional historical information unavailable. The *Topkapi Muzesi Mudurlugu* in Istanbul, where the Crown Jewels are kept, recently denied ownership of these two stones.

Vanderbilt

A 16.25-carat, pear-shaped engagement ring, given by Reginald Vanderbilt to Gloria Morgan in 1922. Pur-

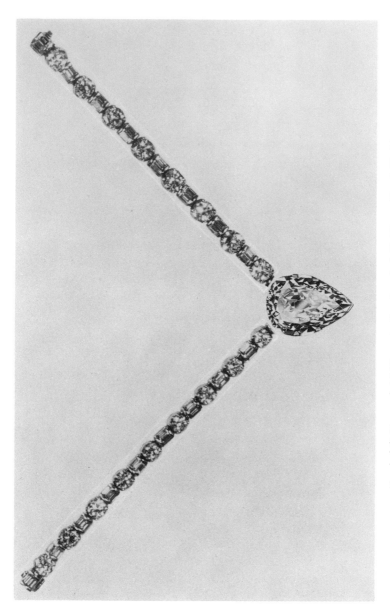

Vanderbilt Diamond. 16.25 carats. Courtesy Jack M. Werst, Miami, Florida

chased from Tiffany's for $75,000. Sold by Mrs. Vanderbilt in 1946 to Jack M. Werst, Miami, Florida, gem dealer, in whose possession it rests today.

Van Zyl

Found at Cawood's Hope, Pniel Estate, South Africa, 1913. 229.25 carats. Present whereabouts unknown.

Vitoria

Found in 1943 on Abaeté River, Minas Gerais, Brazil. 328.34 carats. Bought by Harry Winston, New York City merchant, and cut into forty-four stones; the largest, 30.39 carats. Final disposition unknown.

Webster Kopje

A South African diamond, found in 1907. 124 carats. Additional information not available.

Yellow Goddess

A 29.50-carat emerald-cut stone, cut from a 100-carat crystal. Shown by a Beverly Hills jeweler in the mid-1950's. Ultimate disposition unknown.

Yubileiny

Found in a pipe at Mirnyy, eastern Siberia, 1956. 32.56 carats. No further facts known.

APPENDIX

Recent and Additional Important Diamonds

The Amsterdam

This rare diamond of African origin is reported to be completely black. A 145-facet pear-shaped stone weighing 33.74 carats was cut from a 55.85-carat rough. The stone was first shown in February, 1973, at D. Drukker & Zn., Amsterdam. Presently the diamond is not for sale, but will be kept as a showpiece for the 700th anniversary of Amsterdam, the "Diamond City."

Baumgold Pears

Two pear-shaped stones weighing 50 carats each were cut from the *Baumgold Rough* which yielded a total of 14 stones. Present owner and location unknown.

Baumgold Rough

This 609.25-carat, bluish-colored rough was found at the Wesselton Mine, South Africa, in 1922. It was acquired in 1923 by Baumgold Brothers, Inc., New York, and 14 stones were cut from it. The largest stones cut were two pear shapes, the *Baumgold Pears*, weighing 50 carats each. There is no record of the size of the other stones, but most of the 14 reportedly were sold in San Francisco.

Briolette of India

The *Briolette of India* is a legendary diamond of 90.38 carats, which, if the fables about it are true, may be the oldest diamond on record, perhaps older than the Koh-i-Noor. In the 12th century, Eleanor of Aquitaine, first Queen of France and later Queen of England, brought the stone to England. Her son, Richard the Lionhearted, is said to have taken it on the Third Crusade.

It next appeared in the 16th century when Henry II of France gave it to his blonde mistress, Diane de Poitiers. It was shown in one of the many portraits of her while at Fontainebleau.

After disappearing for four centures, the stone surfaced again in 1950 when the jeweler Harry Winston, of New York,

The Briolette of India. 90.38 carats. Courtesy Harry Winston, Inc., New York City.

The Amsterdam Diamond. 33.74 carats. Courtesy D. Drukker & Zn., Amsterdam.

bought it from an Indian Maharajah. It was resold to Mrs. I. W. Killam and bought back by Mr. Winston, following her death, about 10 years later.

In 1970, Mr. Winston showed the stone at the Diamond Dinner for American Fashion Editors.

Byfield

In February, 1971, Parke-Bernet Galleries, New York, sold this large 54.74-carat diamond, set in a ring, to the late Vala Byfield.

Carbonado do Sergio

The *Carbonado do Sergio*, the largest known carbonado, weighing 3,167 carats, was discovered in 1905 at Brejo da Lama, Municipio de Lençois, Bahia, Brazil.

Carbonado Xique-Xique

A 931.6-carat carbonado that was found at Andaraí Lavras, Diamantina, State of Bahia, Brazil. Alternate spelling is *Chique-Chique Diamond.*

Casco de Burro

This 2,000-carat carbonado was discovered in the Municipio de Lençois, Bahia, Brazil.

Constantin

A 46.05-carat emerald-cut diamond of outstanding quality was sold by Christie's, Geneva, in 1970 for an undisclosed sum. Now privately owned, it has been christened *Constantin.* No additional details are known.

Copenhagen Blue

This 45.85-carat emerald-cut blue diamond was fashioned from a rough discovered at the Premier Mine, South Africa. It was named the *Copenhagen Blue* by Danish jewelers during an exhibition in Copenhagen in 1960. Its present owner and location are unknown.

Cotton Belt Star

The *Cotton Belt Star*, a 11.92-carat rough, was reportedly discovered by a 14-month-old baby while her parents were on a diamond digging search at Pine Bluff, Arkansas. The baby, Mary Rogers, is said to have placed a shiny object in her mouth. Much to her parents' delight, it became known as the *Cotton Belt Star* rough.

Earth Star

This 111.59-carat coffee-brown pear shape was cut from a 248.90-carat rough found in the Jagersfontein Mine, South Africa, in 1967. It is thought to be the largest brown diamond in the world and was exhibited along with many other notable diamonds in the "De Beers Hall" of the mining museum at Kimberley in 1971.

Earth Star. 111.59 carats. Courtesy
Baumgold Bros., Inc., New York City.

Eugenie Blue

Believed to have been owned by Empress Eugenie, this 31-carat heart-shaped diamond now resides at the Smithsonian Institution. It was purchased from Harry Winston of New York by Mrs. Merriweather Post, who subsequently donated it to the Smithsonian.

Fifty Years of Aeroflot

Named in commemoration of Soviet Aviation Day, this diamond, weighing 232 carats, was found in the diamond fields at Mirnyy in the Yakutskaya region of Siberia. Discovered in August 1973, it became the largest known Soviet diamond. Within three months, however, another diamond of identical weight, 232 carats, was reportedly found in the same area. This second stone, named *The Star of Yakutiya*, now shares in the honor of the largest Soviet diamond.

Golconda d'Or

This historical stone, considered to be the largest emerald-cut golden diamond in the world, was recut by Asscher of

Amsterdam from its original 130 carats and now weighs 95.40 carats. The *Golconda d'Or* is notable because it is one of the last large diamonds taken from the old Golconda Mines of India.

First mentioned in 1739 as part of the booty taken from Delhi by the Persian invader Nadir Shah, it reportedly was later handed down to the Sultan of Turkey in the early 19th century. In 1909, the first President of the Turkish Republic, Kemal Ataturk, sold the *Golconda d'Or* to a wealthy Turkish family. It was later purchased by Dunklings, the Jewelers, Melbourne, Australia, in 1962 where it is now on permanent display.

Gornyak

The *Gornyak* rough reportedly weighs 44 carats and is valued at 100,000 rubles. It was found in Yakutiya, Siberia, and presently is in the Russian Diamond Fund, Moscow.

Great Brazilian

This 130-carat diamond was once part of the Crown Jewels of Portugal. In 1956 it was claimed to have been set in a $1,250,000 diamond necklace and exhibited at Sears Roebuck stores. Its present owner and location are unknown.

Halphen

Streeter gives the only known record of this diamond: "Almost the only specimen of Red Diamond is a gem of a carat weight, bought by the author and sold to the late Mr. George Samuel for £800."

Iranians

A study of the Crown Jewels of Iran in 1966 by Dr. V. B. Meen and Dr. A. D. Tushingham revealed that there were 23 large diamonds which have been named the "Iranians." Also, there are several other large diamonds, weighing less than 50 carats, in the collection that are not listed here.

There are 19 yellow stones of South African origin which

188

were probably acquired in 1889 by Shah Nasir ud-Din during his trip to Europe. Four diamonds that may be of Indian origin include Iranian 19, 22 and 23, which are white stones, and Iranian 20, a peach-colored diamond.

Iranian 23, weighing 38.18 carats, is thought by some experts to be the *Hornby,* which was described by Edwin Streeter in 1882.

The Iranian listed carat weights, shapes, and colors are as follows:

1 — 152.16; rectangular old brilliant; silver cape
2 — 135.45; high (old) cushion brilliant; cape
3 — 123.93; high (old) cushion brilliant; silver cape
4 — 121.90; multi-faceted octahedron; cape
5 — 114.28; high (old) cushion brilliant; silver cape
6 — 86.61; rounded triangular brilliant; cape
7 — 86.28; irregular Mogul cut; silver cape
8 — 78.96; high (old) cushion brilliant; cape
9 — 75.29; high (old) cushion brilliant; cape
10 — 75.00 (est.); pendeloque brilliant; silver cape
11 — 75.00 (est.); pendeloque brilliant; silver cape
12 — 72.84; irregular pear shape; champagne
13 — 65.65; rectangular (old) brilliant; cape
14 — 60.00 (est.); cushion brilliant; yellow
15 — 57.85; round brilliant; silver cape
16 — 57.15; cushion brilliant; silver cape
17 — 56.19; cushion brilliant; silver cape
18 — 55.67; cushion brilliant; silver cape
19 — 54.58; irregular oval Mogul cut; colorless
20 — 54.35; high (old) cushion brilliant; peach
21 — 53.50; high (old) cushion brilliant; silver cape
22 — 51.90; elliptical Mogul cut; colorless
23 — 38.18; multi-faceted trapezoid cut; colorless

Krupp

The 33.19-carat emerald-cut *Krupp* diamond was once part of the estate of Vera Krupp, ex-wife of the German munition

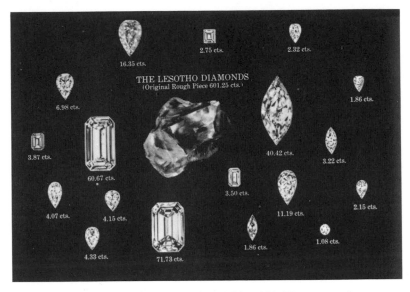

The Lesotho Diamond rough weighing 601.25 carats and the 18 stones cut from it. Courtesy Harry Winston, Inc., New York City.

maker and industrialist. In 1968 it was sold at auction by Parke-Bernet for $305,000 to Richard Burton for his wife, Elizabeth Taylor.

Lesotho

The *Lesotho Diamond* was discovered in Lesotho, Africa, in May 1967 by Mrs. Ernestine Ramoboa at the Letseng-le-Draai diggings. The brownish colored rough weighed 601.25 carats and was sold for $302,400 at auction in Maseru, the capital of Lesotho, to a South African dealer. He in turn sold it to a European dealer. This diamond was later purchased in Geneva by Harry S. Winston of New York who subsequently cut it into 18 stones, totaling 242.50 carats, in 1969. Most diamond cutting styles are represented. An emerald-cut diamond of 71.73 carats is the largest stone cut from the *Lesotho* rough. Reportedly all have been sold to private owners.

Lesotho B

This large rough weighing 527 carats was one of the three largest diamonds ever found in Lesotho. It was discovered in 1965 and bought by Mr. E. J. Serafini of Bloemfontein and Maseru for $162,400. The *Lesotho B* was later resold to an unknown American dealer in Antwerp. Present disposition is not known.

Lesotho C

Discovered at the Kao diggings, Lesotho, in 1967, this large brown rough weighing 338 carats was initially sold for $54,740. It was reportedly cut into ten stones in Amsterdam. The largest gem is a 24-carat marquise. The whereabouts of these diamonds is unknown today.

Maria

Maria Komemkima discovered this 106-carat rough at Yakutskaya, Siberia, in 1966. At that time, it was the largest diamond found in the Soviet Union. The *Maria* is now in the Russian Diamond Fund, Moscow.

Maxwell

This greenish colored rough weighing 3 carats was discovered in 1863 at Morgan County, Indiana. It was reported to be owned by Mr. Maxwell of Martinsville, Indiana.

Mounce

The *Mounce* rough, weighing 18.20 carats, is the tenth largest diamond found in the United States. It was discovered in 1969 by a girl playing in her yard at Princeton, Louisiana. C. E. Mounce, a Shreveport jeweler, purchased the stone and had it cut by Lazare Kaplan & Sons into three stones. A 3.47-carat oval, the largest stone, was named the *La. Mounce* and retained by Mr. Mounce. A 2.75-carat heart shape and a 2.27-carat marquise were sold for an undisclosed sum to unknown buyers.

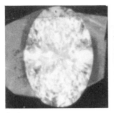

(c)

(a)　　　　　　　　(b)

Mounce Diamonds. (a) 3.47-carat oval; (b) 2.75-carat heart shape; (c) 2.27 carat marquise. GIA photo not to scale.

Mounce Rough. 18.20 carats. GIA photo

Nawanger

The 148-carat brilliant-cut *Nawanger* diamond was owned in 1970 by the Maharanee Gulabkumberba of Nawanger. It is reported to have come from Russia.

Nooitgedacht

The *Nooitgedacht* yellow diamond rough weighing 325 carats was discovered by a native in the diggings at Nooitgedacht, near Kimberley, Cape Province, South Africa, in 1953. The site had been dug for 22 years without success by its owner, Christoffel Boer. The diamond was sold by Boer for $38,000, and the discoverer was awarded $840. The disposition of the *Nooitgedacht* is not known.

Red Diamond

Discovered in 1927 at the Lichtenberg diggings of South Africa, the 33-carat black bort rough sold for only $160. Originally thought to be just a piece of bort to be used as powder for polishing, the buyer, Mr. Houtakker, took the advice of Sir Ernest Oppenheimer and sent the rough to Amsterdam for cutting. There, a flawless blood-red emerald-cut stone of 5.05 carats was cut from the center of the rough.

The *Red Diamond* had many adventures and was first sold in 1947 for an unknown price. In 1968 it was reported to be owned by a private collector in New York.

Rojtman

This large 107.46-carat yellow diamond was exhibited at the De Beers Diamond Pavilion in Johannesburg in 1966 by its owner, Mrs. Marc Rojtman of New York. Prior to the acquisition of the *Rojtman* diamond by the late Mr. Marc Rojtman, nothing is known of its history. Some experts believe that it is similar to the *Star of Diamonds*, a high-quality South African diamond found in the early days of the diamond fields.

Spoonmaker's

The *Spoonmaker's* diamond is an 84-carat pear shape set in a double frame of 49 smaller diamonds. It is one of the chief treasures of the Topkapi Museum of Istanbul. There is some evidence that the *Spoonmaker's* and *Turkey II* may be the same diamond.

Stalingrad

The 166-carat *Stalingrad* rough was found near Mirnyy, Yakutskaya, Siberia, in 1968. It is also known as the *Siberian* and presently is on exhibit at the Russian Diamond Fund in the Kremlin.

Star of Denmark

This 34.29-carat canary diamond was cut from a 105-carat rough found in 1885 at the Kimberley Mine, South Africa. The Princess of Denmark gave the stone set in a ring to Queen Kapiolani of Hawaii for the Queen Victoria Jubilee in 1887. Its present owner is reported to be Frank Spenger, Sr. of Berkeley, California.

Star of Sierra Leone Rough. 969.8 carats.
Courtesy Harry Winston, Inc., New York City.

Star of Murfreesboro

This diamond is the largest ever found by a tourist at the "Crater of Diamonds," Murfreesboro, Arkansas. It was discovered on March 1, 1964 by John L. Pollock of Columbus, Georgia, and weighed 35.25 carats in the rough. The *Star of Murfreesboro* is blue in color and of an odd rounded crystal form which lacks the typical faces of a diamond.

Star of Sierra Leone

The *Star of Sierra Leone* is the third largest rough diamond ever discovered and the second largest discovered in this century. It was found on February 14, 1972, at the separator plant of the Diminco Mine at Yengema, Sierra Leone. Although at 969.8 carats it ranks below the Cullinan (3,106 carats) and the Excelsior (995.20 carats) in total weight, it is the largest alluvial diamond ever discovered.

The *Star of Sierra Leone* was purchased by Harry Winston, New York, who is now cutting the diamond. To date, a 140-carat emerald cut has been fashioned. No additional finished gems have been reported as yet.

Star of Texas

The *Star of Texas*, a 48.19-carat, sherry-colored round diamond, was named by the Linz Brothers of Dallas, Texas, in 1971. It is of African origin and was cut in Belgium. Present disposition is unknown.

Star of the East

The *Star of the East*, believed to be of Indian origin, was once owned by Sultan Abdul Hamid II of Turkey, who also owned the famous blue *Hope* diamond. In 1908, this 94.80-carat pear shape was purchased by Mrs. Evelyn Walsh McLean, who also owned the *Hope* diamond. The *Star of the East* was bought by Harry Winston from the jewel estate of Mrs. McLean in 1949. It was reportedly in the possession of King Farouk of Egypt at the time he went into exile.

Star of Yakutiya

This diamond weighing 232 carats was the second of two large diamonds of identical weight reported to have been found in the diamond fields at Mirnyy in the Yakutskaya region of Siberia in 1973. Scarcely three months after the *Fifty Years of Aeroflot* diamond became the largest Soviet diamond on record, the *Star of Yakutiya* was found and now shares equally in the honor.

Sterns Diamond

In October 1973, a 223.6-carat fine quality yellow octahedron diamond was picked up by a crusher attendant, Mr. Andrew Moraladi, in the recovery plant of the Dutoitspan Mine, Kimberley. The Sterns Diamond Organization acquired the diamond from the Johannesburg diamond cutting factory of O. Kagan and Company. Three stones have been cut: the *Sterns Star*, a round brilliant of 85.93 carats, is the largest diamond reportedly polished in South Africa; two other stones have been cut, one an emerald cut weighing 21.04 carats and the other a marquise weighing 6.08 carats.

Tai Hang Star

This 60-carat stone was cut from a 120-carat rough found at the Kimberley Mine by Michael Abrahams of Johannesburg. No other information is available on this large diamond.

Taylor-Burton Diamond

This pear-shaped 69.42-carat diamond was cut by Harry Winston, New York, from a 240.80-carat rough found in 1966 at the Premier Mine, South Africa. Mr. Winston sold the stone in 1967 for an undisclosed sum to Mrs. Walter Ames, sister of Walter Annenberg, a well-known publisher.

In 1969, Cartier of New York bought the stone for $1,050,000 at the Parke-Bernet Galleries auction in New York. It was christened the *Cartier* diamond and resold the following day for an undisclosed sum to Richard Burton for his wife, Elizabeth Taylor. The diamond has subsequently been renamed the *Taylor-Burton*.

Toktogul

The *Toktogul* was reported to have been found at Mirnyy, Yakutskaya, Siberia, sometime after 1955. This 37.56-carat rough is presently in the Russian Diamond Fund at the Kremlin.

Transvaal Blue

The *Transvaal Blue* pear shape weighs 25 carats. It was cut from a rough found in the Premier Mine, Transvaal. Its present owners are the Baumgold Brothers.

Valentina Tereshkova

The *Valentina Tereshkova* was named for the first woman cosmonaut. The rough crystal weighs 51 carats and was valued at $63,900 in 1968. It is presently in the Russian Diamond Fund.

Transvaal Blue. 25 carats. Courtesy
Baumgold Bros., Inc., New York City.

Windsorten

This 140-carat rough was found in 1961 by J. J. Steyn at the Windsorten Breakwater on the Vaal River, South Africa. Steyn reportedly sold the rough to a Johannesburg cutter for $26,880. Ultimate disposition unknown.

Winston

The *Winston* diamond is a flawless 62.50-carat pear shape gem measuring one and one-half inches long and one inch wide. The colorless rough was found in the Jagersfontein Mine, South Africa, in 1952. In 1953, Harry Winston purchased it in London for $230,800. It was subsequently cut and sold to a "certain King of Saudi Arabia" and later returned to Winston who, in turn, resold it shortly thereafter to a private owner in Canada.

The Zale Light of Peace Diamond (130.27 carats) and 12 satellite stones weighing 42.19 carats. Courtesy Zale Corporation, Dallas, Texas.

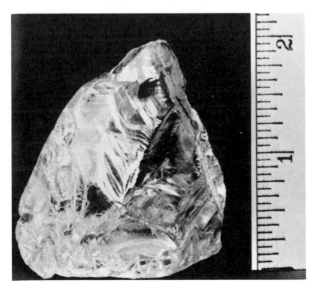

The Zale Light of Peace Rough. 434.60 carats. Courtesy Zale Corporation, Dallas, Texas

Young

The 1.66-carat silver cape *Young* diamond rough was discovered in 1898 in Brown County, Indiana. It is currently at the Smithsonian Institution.

Zale Light of Peace

The 434.60-carat rough stone that yielded the 130.27-carat *Zale Light of Peace* diamond was purchased for an undisclosed sum by Zale Corporation in 1969 on the European rough diamond market. One of the largest known diamonds to be cut in the United States, the *Zale Light of Peace* is thought to have come from Sierra Leone in western Africa. The rough was 2 inches long, 1-3/4 inches wide, and produced a total of 172.46 carats of gems, with a loss in cutting of 262.14 carats. Thirteen stones were cut from the rough. The largest stone, called the *Zale Light of Peace*, is a pear shape weighing 130.27 carats. The dozen satellites, ranging from a 0.37-carat pear shape to the almost perfectly matched 9.04- and 9.11-carat marquises, weigh a total of 42.19 carats.

The Zale Corporation, owner of the diamonds, reported that the *Zale Light of Peace* and the 12 satellite stones will not be sold for a ten-year period. During this time, the stones will be exhibited on behalf of charitable organizations for fund-raising purposes.

Zlata Prata

This Russian diamond is reported to have been found in Yakutskaya, Siberia, sometime after 1955. The rough weighs 38.72 carats and presently is in the Russian Diamond Fund in the Kremlin.

"616" (unnamed) Diamond. 616 carats. Courtesy DeBeers Consolidated Mines, Limited.

Taylor-Burton Diamond 69.42 carats. Courtesy N. W. Ayer & Sons, Inc., New York City.

"616" (Unnamed)

On April 15, 1974, Mr. Abel Maretela, an African worker, discovered a 616-carat yellow octahedron at the Dutoitspan Mine. This is the 9th largest diamond ever recorded and the largest ever found at Kimberley. The yellow octahedron is of good shape but not of the best quality. Mr. Maretela was duly rewarded for the find.

This big rough will not be sold. De Beers Consolidated Mines has placed this large diamond on permanent display in the De Beers Hall at the Open Mine Museum in Kimberley.

THE GEMOLOGICAL INSTITUTE OF AMERICA

Founded in 1931 by Robert M. Shipley, the Gemological Institute of America, known to most jewelers as GIA or the Institute, is the educational, research and testing center of the jewelry industry. The purpose of this endowed, nonprofit organization is to provide professional training and other services primarily for jewelers, and also for gem hobbyists. But the ultimate beneficiary is the public, because the jeweler's knowledge means consumer protection.

EDUCATIONAL ACTIVITIES

The Institute's training is provided in several different ways: on a home-study, or correspondence, basis, by classroom instruction, or partly by correspondence and partly in residence.

Correspondence courses are offered on *Diamonds, Colored Stones, Gem Identification, Pearls, Jewelry Retailing, Jewelry Designing,* and *Creative Jewelry Display.*

One-week classes in *Diamond Appraisal, Gem Identification,* and *Jewelry Designing,* two week classes in *Diamond Setting* and *Jewelry Repair* are conducted in major cities throughout the United States, and some are given abroad.

PUBLISHING

Another service is publishing. *Gems & Gemology*, a professional quarterly in the field of gems and related subjects, has been published since 1934. A number of books have also been published, including dictionaries, texts and other books and articles of particular interest to gemologists and jewelers. In addition to this book, some of the titles include *The Jeweler's Manual*, *The Diamond Dictionary*, *Dictionary of Gems and Gemology*, and *Handbook of Gem Identification*.

After successful completion of the *Diamond Course*, the *Diamond Certificate* is awarded, or if the *Colored Stone* and *Gem Identification Courses* are completed, the *Colored Stone Certificate* is awarded. When all three are completed successfully, the *Gemologist Diploma* is conferred. The *Graduate Gemologist Diploma* is given upon successful completion of the Institute's three Gemology correspondence courses and two short residence classes. One who holds the *Graduate Gemologist in Residence Diploma* has completed successfully the entire gemology curriculum in an intensive, 6-month's full-time program in GIA's Santa Monica or New York facilities.

THE GIA GEM-TRADE LABORATORIES

The GIA Gem-Trade Laboratories in Los Angeles, New York City and Santa Monica provide complete testing and grading facilities for jewelers and the public. In addition to gem testing, grading and determination of extent and cause of damage, they develop identification methods for new gemstone organizations, including U.S. Customs, the FBI, Better Business Bureaus, the Jewelers' Vigilance Committee, Chambers of Commerce and insurance companies.

SPECIAL INSTRUMENTS

A wholly-owned subsidiary of the Institute designs and manufactures professional gem-testing and gem-merchandising instruments. Included in the equipment familiar to most jewelers are GEM's Mark V, Gemolite, Gem Detector, Diamond Grader, Illuminator Polariscope, Duplex II Refractometer, DiamondLite, Spectroscope Unit, Diamondlux, ProportionScope, and Mini-Lab. Gem Instruments Corporation has the services of the talented designers Kenneth M. Moore and Gale M. Johnson.

TECHNICAL & TEACHING STAFF

The technical and teaching staff of the Institute consists of specialists who are trained and experienced in one or more of the fields of jewelry marketing, the sciences, education and designing. Its policy-setting body is its jeweler-scientist member Board of Governors, elected annually.

The President is Richard T. Liddicoat, Jr., who directs the different branches of the organization from its Santa Monica Headquarters. The Board of Governors and other officers, except for the President and Assistant Secretary, serve without compensation. Arthur F. Gleim is Chairman of the Board; George Kaplan, Vice Chairman; and Stanley E. Church, Secretary-Treasurer.

There are over 75 Graduate Gemologists on GIA's staff of approximately 200 people. Robert Earnest is Dean of Resident Students in Santa Monica; Charles Fryer is Supervisor of the Laboratory there; George P. Yantzer is the Director of the Los Angeles Laboratory; Dennis Foltz is Correspondence Course Supervisor, R.A.P. Gaal, Ph.D. is Associate Editor of Gems & Gemology and also is in charge of correspondence course and publications' revisions; and Vince Manson, Ph.D. is in charge

203

of physical research. Resident Course Instructors include William Boyajian, Archie Curtis, Jill Fisher, Jim Lucey, Ray Page, and many more.

J. Michael Allbritton is in charge of the one-week classes in Diamond Grading and Appraising and Gem Identification and is assisted by Janice Mack. A. Richard Shalberg is in charge of the Jewelry Craft Classes. Among other long term key administrative employees are T.J. Barrows and Margaret Orozco; Raymond Ouderkirk is Comptroller.

The staff of the Eastern Division includes Robert Crowningshield, Director of the New York Gem Trade Laboratory; Bertram Krashes, Assistant Director; Eunice Miles, staff gemologist; and instructors John Cubitto, Paul Holt, Dennis Maun, David Fowler, Ingrid Nolte, and many others plus several administrative aides.

FACILITIES

GIA has three locations. Its modern Headquarters building is located at 1660 Stewart Street, Santa Monica, California 90404. The Eastern Division, including the New York Gem-Trade Laboratory, maintains offices and classrooms at 580 Fifth Avenue, New York, New York 10036. The Los Angeles Laboratory is located at 606 South Olive Street, Los Angeles, California 90014. The home-study courses are conducted from the West Coast. Instructors from the Santa Monica and New York facilities conduct the one and two-week classes throughout the nation and abroad. The full-time residence classes are given in Santa Monica and New York to students from all over the world.